ESSENTIAL LIFE SKILLS FOR YOUNG ADULTS

LEARN THE SKILLS YOU NEED FOR INDEPENDENCE,
CONFIDENCE, AND SUCCESS IN THE REAL-WORLD

AL PARKER

BONUS CHAPTER: PARENT TALK

TABLE OF CONTENTS

INTRODUCTION

As a young adult, fresh out of high school, I faced a moment that felt like the edge of a cliff. I had to decide whether to go to college, start working, or take a different path altogether. I had the grades, the support, and the drive, but I felt like I needed help. I didn't know how to navigate the everyday challenges of adulthood. It was a time filled with uncertainty and a bit of fear. Many young adults find themselves standing at this very edge, looking at the vast expanse of the future, unsure how to take the next step.

This book is not just a resource, but a lifeline for young adults and their parents. It's a beacon of hope, equipping you with practical life skills that foster independence, confidence, and success in the real world. These skills serve as the foundation for navigating the complexities of adulthood with clarity and assurance, ensuring you're well-prepared for what's to come.

The vision for this book is simple yet profound. It offers practical guidance and frameworks for decision-making, empowering you to take charge of your life confidently. Think of this book as a rite of passage, much like a Bar mitzvah or a quinceañera. These ceremonies mark the transition into adulthood, filled with lessons and traditions that prepare you for the responsibilities ahead. Similarly, this book aims to equip you with the skills and knowledge you need to thrive.

This book is a valuable resource for young adults and their parents, helping them transition into the real world. It's more than just a book; it's a bridge that offers insights and tools to foster a shared understanding and approach to the challenges and opportunities that lie ahead. Parents, this book is designed to help you support your children's transition into adulthood, providing you with the knowledge and tools to guide them effectively. It's a journey we can all take together, supporting each other and strengthening our bond.

Let me give you a brief overview of what you can expect from this book. Each chapter is meticulously structured to focus on a different aspect of life skills. We start with understanding and managing your finances, helping you to budget, save, and invest wisely. Next, we move on to building solid relationships, emphasizing communication and empathy. The following chapters cover essential skills like time management, goal setting, and problem-solving. We also address the importance of self-care and mental health, ensuring you have a balanced approach to life. Finally, we explore career development, offering tips on job searching, networking, and workplace success. This structured approach will guide you through adulthood's various challenges and opportunities.

My passion for helping young adults and parents is deeply rooted in my journey. I've experienced the struggles and triumphs of transitioning into adulthood firsthand. With a background in education and counseling, I've gained a profound understanding of these challenges. I've dedicated my career to helping young people find their footing and thrive in their adult lives.

Please actively engage with the content of this book. Apply the skills daily, experiment with the frameworks, and share your experiences with others. This book is not just a collection of theories and advice; it's a practical guide you can use daily. Your active participation is not just encouraged; it's vital. It will not only enhance your learning but also contribute to the collective wisdom of our community. You'll be surprised at how much you can learn from one another and how much your voice matters.

As you read through these pages, remember that this journey is about growth and learning. You will face challenges, and there will be moments of doubt. But each step you take is a step toward becoming a more confident and capable individual. Embrace the journey with an open heart and mind, and know that you have the power to shape your future.

So, here's to you, standing at the edge of a new beginning. Let's take this journey together, one step at a time. The skills you learn here will be your compass, guiding you through adulthood's vast and exciting landscape. This book is not just a guide; it's a companion that will empower you to navigate the challenges and opportunities of adulthood with confidence and clarity. Welcome to the adventure of your life.

1

FINANCIAL LITERACY AND INDEPENDENCE

S tanding in line at the grocery store, my friend Sarah glanced at the total on the register and realized she had left her wallet at home. She quickly pulled out her phone to check her bank balance, only to find her account nearly empty. Panic set in. This wasn't the first time she found herself in a financial bind. Despite working full-time, Sarah struggled with managing her money, often running out before her next paycheck. She had no budget, no plan, and each month felt like a financial rollercoaster. Many young adults, like Sarah, face similar challenges. They earn money but lack the skills to manage it effectively, leading to stress and financial instability. This lack of financial management can lead to missed opportunities, debt, and constant worry about the future.

This chapter is all about helping you gain control over your finances through budgeting. Financial literacy is understanding and using various financial skills, including personal financial management, budgeting, and investing. It's a crucial part of achieving independence and success. With a solid understanding of managing your money, it's easier to avoid falling into debt, miss out on savings opportunities, and feel anxious about the future. By learning to budget, you can track your income and expenses, save money, and plan for long-term goals. Budgeting is not just a tool; it's a key to financial stability and confidence.

1.1 BUDGETING BASICS: HOW TO CREATE AND STICK TO A BUDGET

Budgeting is more than just a financial tool; it's a life skill that empowers you to make informed decisions about your money. Without a budget, you may find yourself constantly wondering where your money went, struggling to pay bills on time, or unable to save for important goals. On the other hand, a well-planned budget brings a sense of relief and peace of mind, reducing financial stress and providing reassurance about your financial stability. It helps you achieve your financial goals and gives you a clear picture of your finances.

Creating a budget starts with identifying your income sources. This includes your salary, freelance work, allowances, or financial aid. Once you know how much money you have coming in, the next step is to categorize your expenses. Expenses can be divided into fixed and variable categories. Fixed expenses, such as rent, utilities, insurance premiums, and loan repayments, remain constant monthly. Variable expenses, like groceries, dining out, entertainment, and travel, can fluctuate. Budgeting tools like spreadsheets or apps like Mint or YNAB can make tracking these expenses easier. These tools allow you to input your income and expenses, categorize them, and visualize where your money is going.

Sticking to a budget requires discipline and regular review. Setting realistic spending limits is crucial. If you place too strict limits, you may find it easier to stick to them. Instead, set achievable goals that still allow for some flexibility. Regularly reviewing and adjusting your budget is also essential. Life is dynamic, and your budget should reflect changes in your income or expenses. Accountability methods, like having a budgeting partner or keeping a financial journal, can help you stay on track. Sharing your goals with someone else can provide motivation and support, making it easier to stick to your budget.

Budget challenges are common but can be managed with the right strategies. Unexpected expenses, such as car repairs or medical bills, can reduce your budget. To handle these, it's essential to have an emergency fund. Start small and gradually build up your savings to cover at least three to six months of living expenses. Avoiding impulse purchases is another crucial strategy. Before purchasing, ask yourself if it's a need or a want. If it's a want, consider waiting a few days before deciding. This approach can help you stay in control of your finances and reduce financial stress.

By mastering the basics of budgeting, you set the foundation for financial independence and success. This skill helps you manage your finances and prepares you for future economic decisions, like buying a home, investing, or starting a family. So, take the time to create a budget, stick to it, and adjust as needed. With a solid budget, you'll find that you can navigate your financial life with greater confidence and ease.

1.2 UNDERSTANDING CREDIT SCORES AND HOW TO BUILD CREDIT

Imagine you're applying for your first apartment. You've found the perfect place, and the landlord seems eager to rent. But then they run a credit check, and your application is denied. Why? Because your credit score is low or non-existent. This scenario is all too common for many young adults who are just starting to navigate the world of credit. A credit score is a numerical representation of your creditworthiness based on your credit history. It affects your ability to secure loans, influences the interest rates you're offered, and even impacts rental applications and job opportunities.

Credit scores typically range from 300 to 850, with higher scores indicating better creditworthiness. When you apply for a loan, whether for a car, a home, or even a personal loan, lenders look at your credit score to determine the risk they're taking by lending you money. A lower score might mean higher interest rates or even loan denial. Similarly, landlords and employers often check credit scores to gauge financial responsibility. A poor score can limit your housing options and job prospects, making it crucial to understand and manage your credit effectively.

Building and maintaining a good credit score is a journey that requires patience and discipline. First, always pay your bills on time. This shows lenders that you're reliable and can manage your financial obligations. Keep your credit card balances low as well. Aim to use at most 30% of your available credit limit. High balances can signal to lenders that you're overextended financially, even if you make your payments on time. Avoid unnecessary credit inquiries; each hard inquiry can temporarily lower your score. Only apply for credit when needed; remember how often you seek new credit. You can build a strong credit history over time by staying focused and disciplined.

Common mistakes can severely damage your credit score. Missing payments is one of the biggest pitfalls. Even one missed payment can have a significant impact. Maxing out your credit cards is another mistake. It affects your credit utilization rate and makes it harder to manage debt. Closing old credit accounts is a good idea, but it can hurt your score by reducing your overall credit history length and available credit. Instead, keep older accounts open and use them occasionally to keep them active.

Monitoring and improving your credit score involves a few proactive steps. Utilize credit monitoring services like Credit Karma or Experian. These services regularly update your credit score and alert you to changes or potential fraud. Periodically review your credit reports for errors. You're entitled to a free report from each of the three major credit bureaus—Equifax, Experian, and TransUnion—once a year through AnnualCreditReport.com. Dispute any inaccuracies you find, as errors can lower your score. By staying vigilant, you can catch and correct issues before they become more significant problems.

Reflection Section: Building Good Credit Habits

Take a moment to reflect on your current credit habits. Do you pay your bills on time? Are you keeping your credit card balances low? Write down three specific actions to improve or maintain your credit score. This might include setting up automatic bill payments, creating a budget to manage spending, or scheduling a monthly review of your credit report. By identifying and committing to these actions, you'll be on your way to building a solid credit foundation.

Understanding and managing your credit score is a vital part of financial literacy. It opens doors to better economic opportunities and helps you confidently navigate adult life's complexities. By taking proactive steps to build and maintain good credit, you set yourself up for a future of financial stability and success.

1.3 SAVING STRATEGIES: BUILDING AN EMERGENCY FUND

Picture this: driving to work, your car suddenly sputters and stops. The mechanic informs you that the repair costs will be hefty. This unexpected expense could change your entire financial plan without an emergency fund. An emergency fund acts as a financial safety net. It protects against unforeseen costs like medical bills, car repairs, or sudden job loss. Having one can lead to high-interest debt or economic stability. The presence of an emergency fund provides peace of mind, knowing you have a cushion to fall back on. It allows you to handle life's curveballs without derailing your financial goals.

Starting an emergency fund may seem daunting, but it's a step-by-step process. Begin by setting a savings goal. Financial experts often recommend having three to six months' worth of living expenses saved up. This amount can cover your essential costs, such as rent, groceries, and utilities, during unexpected financial strain. Once you have a goal in mind, automate your savings. Set up a direct deposit from your paycheck to a separate savings account. By automating this process, you ensure consistent contributions without thinking about it. Additional income sources can also help you build your fund faster. Consider taking on a part-time job, freelancing, or selling unused items. Every bit adds up, accelerating your progress toward a fully funded emergency account.

Maintaining your emergency fund is as crucial as building it. Keep the fund in a separate, easily accessible account. This ensures you can quickly access the money when needed but prevents you from dipping into it for non-emergencies. Replenish the fund after use. If you withdraw money for an emergency, prioritize rebuilding your fund to its original level. Avoid using the emergency fund for non-urgent expenses. Using this money for a vacation or a new gadget might be tempting, but doing so defeats the purpose of having a safety net.

Real-life examples can be inspiring and motivational. Consider the story of a young professional who faced a sudden job loss. Because she had diligently built an emergency fund, she could cover her living expenses for several months while searching for a new job. This financial cushion allowed her to focus on finding the correct position without the pressure of immediate financial need. Another example is a family that used its emergency fund to cover unexpected medical expenses. The fund prevented them from going into debt and provided the financial stability needed during a challenging time.

Case Study: The Impact of an Emergency Fund

Reflect on a college student who saved diligently during part-time jobs. When his car broke down unexpectedly, his emergency fund covered the repair costs, allowing him to continue commuting to classes without financial stress. This experience reinforced the importance of having a financial safety net and motivated him to keep building his fund even after graduation.

These real-life stories highlight the importance and benefits of having an emergency fund. They show how preparation can turn potential financial crises into manageable inconveniences. Following practical steps and maintaining discipline, you can build and sustain an emergency fund, providing economic security and peace of mind. Knowing you have a financial cushion allows you to face life's uncertainties confidently, ensuring unexpected expenses don't derail your financial stability.

1.4 INVESTING 101: STARTING SMALL AND GROWING YOUR WEALTH

When I first heard about investing, it seemed like a concept reserved for the wealthy or financially savvy. But the truth is, investing is crucial for anyone looking to build wealth over time, and it's vital for young adults. Unlike saving, which involves setting aside money for future use, investing allows your money to grow by earning returns over time. This growth is primarily powered by compound interest, where you earn interest not just on your initial investment but also on the accumulated interest over time. Imagine planting a tree that grows and produces seeds that grow into more trees. This is the magic of compound interest, and it's why starting to invest early can significantly impact your financial future.

The investing world might seem overwhelming for beginners, but a few key options are accessible and practical. Stocks represent shares of ownership in a company and have the potential for high returns, though they come with higher risk. On the other hand, bonds are loans you give to a corporation or government in exchange for periodic interest payments and the return of the bond's face value at maturity. They are generally considered safer than stocks but offer lower returns. Mutual funds and Exchange-Traded Funds (ETFs) pool money from many investors to purchase a diversified portfolio of stocks, bonds, or other securities. These funds provide diversification, which reduces risk by spreading investments across various assets. Retirement accounts such as IRAs and 401(k)s are also excellent investment vehicles. They offer tax advantages that can significantly boost your savings over time. For example, contributions to a traditional IRA may be tax-deductible, and the investments grow tax-deferred until you withdraw the money in retirement.

Investing with limited funds is entirely possible and is straightforward. Micro-investing apps like Acorns and Robinhood allow you to begin investing with small amounts of money. Acorns, for instance, round up your everyday purchases to the nearest dollar and invest the spare change. This means you can start building your portfolio without needing much money upfront. Setting up automatic contributions to your investment accounts is another effective strategy. By automating your investments, you ensure consistent contributions, taking advantage of dollar-cost averaging, which involves regularly investing a fixed amount regardless of market conditions. This strategy mitigates the impact of market volatility and reduces the risk of making poorly timed investments. Diversifying your investments is also crucial. Rather than putting all your money into one stock or asset, spread it across various investments to minimize risk. This way, if one investment underperforms, others may offset the loss.

While investing can be rewarding, it's essential to avoid common mistakes that can undermine your efforts. Market timing, or trying to predict when to buy or sell investments to maximize returns, is a risky strategy that often leads to poor results. Instead, focus on a long-term investment strategy. Another pitfall is concentrating all your money on one stock or asset. Diversification protects you from significant losses if a single investment performs poorly. Overlooking fees and taxes is another common mistake. Investment fees and taxes can affect your returns, so knowing these costs and seeking out low-fee investment options is essential. For example, many mutual funds have expense ratios that cover management and administrative costs. Opting for low-cost index funds, which aim to replicate the performance of a market index, can help you keep more of your returns.

Reflection Section: Your First Investment Steps

Think about what you want to achieve with your investments. Are you saving for retirement, a home, or another long-term goal? Write down your investment goals and the steps you'll take to start investing. This might include opening an investment account, setting up automatic contributions, or researching investment options. Reflecting on your objectives and planning your first steps can make the process more manageable and concrete.

1.5 NAVIGATING STUDENT LOANS: HOW TO MANAGE AND PAY OFF DEBT

Understanding student loans is crucial for anyone pursuing higher education. Federal and private loans have distinct features that can significantly impact your financial future. Federal loans, offered by the government, generally come with lower interest rates and more flexible repayment options. They can be further categorized into subsidized and unsubsidized loans. Subsidized loans are particularly beneficial because the government pays the interest while you're in school, during grace periods, and deferment.

On the other hand, unsubsidized loans accrue interest when the loan is disbursed, increasing the total amount you'll have to repay. Private loans, offered by banks and other financial institutions, often come with higher interest rates and fewer repayment options. These loans can be either fixed-rate, where the interest rate remains constant, or variable-rate, where the rate can change based on market conditions. Understanding these differences can help you make informed decisions about borrowing and repayment.

Managing student loan payments can feel overwhelming, but several strategies can make it more manageable. Setting up automatic payments is a simple yet effective way to ensure you never miss a payment, which can help you avoid late fees and protect your credit score. Many loan servicers offer a slight interest rate reduction if you enroll in automatic payments, providing an added incentive. Exploring repayment plans is another crucial step. Income-driven repayment plans, for instance, cap your monthly payments at a percentage of your discretionary income, making them more affordable. These plans also offer loan forgiveness after a certain number of qualifying payments, which can be a lifeline for those with high debt levels. Making extra payments when possible can also reduce the principal faster, shortening the repayment period and eventually saving you money on interest. Every little bit helps, whether an extra $20 monthly or a lump sum from a holiday bonus.

Several actionable steps expedite the process if you aim to pay off student loans faster. Refinancing your student loans can lower your interest rate, reducing the total amount you owe. This option is particularly beneficial if you have high-interest private loans or your credit score has improved since you first took out the loans. Side jobs or gigs dedicated to loan repayment can also accelerate your progress. Whether freelancing, tutoring, or delivering food, dedicating extra income to your loans can make a significant difference. Applying windfalls, such as tax refunds or work bonuses, directly to your loan principal is another effective strategy. These lump-sum payments can substantially reduce the total interest you'll pay over the life of the loan, helping you become debt-free faster.

Various resources can assist you in managing student debt more effectively. Student loan calculators are invaluable for understanding how different repayment strategies impact your loan balance and payoff timeline. Websites like StudentAid.gov offer calculators to help you compare repayment plans and estimate monthly payments. Loan consolidation programs can simplify your repayment process by combining multiple federal loans into a single loan with one monthly payment. This can make it easier to manage your debt, though it's crucial to understand how consolidation might affect your interest rate and repayment term. Financial counseling services can provide personalized advice and support, helping you navigate complex repayment options and develop a strategy tailored to your financial situation. Many non-profit organizations offer free or low-cost counseling services for student loan borrowers, making it accessible to those who need it most.

Navigating student loans requires a clear understanding of your options and proactive management strategies. By familiarizing yourself with the different types of loans, setting up automatic payments, exploring repayment plans, and utilizing available resources, you can manage your student debt effectively and work towards financial freedom.

1.6 FINANCIAL TOOLS AND APPS: MAKING TECHNOLOGY WORK FOR YOU

In today's digital age, managing your finances has always been challenging, thanks to many financial tools and apps designed to simplify every aspect of economic management. Imagine having a personal financial advisor right in your pocket, guiding you every step of the way. Budgeting apps like YNAB (You Need A Budget) help you track your spending, set goals, and stay on top of your finances. With intuitive interfaces and real-time updates, these apps make budgeting more manageable. Investment platforms such as Robinhood and Betterment offer user-friendly ways to start investing, even if you're new to the game. These platforms provide educational resources and automated services to help you make informed investment decisions. Meanwhile, credit monitoring services like Credit Karma keep you updated on your credit score, alerting you to any changes and helping you improve your credit health. These tools empower you to take control of your financial life confidently and efficiently.

Choosing the right financial apps for your needs involves considering several factors. User-friendliness is paramount. An app with a complicated interface can be discouraging, especially if you're new to financial management. Look for apps with clean, intuitive designs that make navigation easy. Cost and fees are also significant. While some apps offer free versions, others may have subscription fees. Weigh the features and benefits against the cost to determine if the investment is worth it. Features and benefits vary widely among apps. Some offer robust budgeting tools, while others focus on investment tracking or credit monitoring. Identify your primary financial needs and select apps that align with those goals. For example, if your primary concern is budgeting, an app like YNAB, which excels in goal setting and tracking, might be the best fit. On the other hand, if you're keen on investing, Robinhood's commission-free trades and user-friendly interface make it an excellent choice for beginners.

Integrating financial tools into your daily life can significantly enhance their effectiveness. Start by setting up notifications and reminders within the apps. These can alert you to bill due dates, low balances, or significant changes in your spending habits, helping you stay on top of your finances without constant manual checks. Syncing your accounts for comprehensive tracking is another powerful feature. You get a holistic view of your financial situation in one place by linking your bank accounts, credit cards, and investment accounts. This comprehensive tracking helps you identify patterns, make informed decisions, and avoid financial pitfalls. Regularly reviewing and updating your financial data is crucial. Set aside time weekly to review your app's reports, check for discrepancies, and adjust your budget or investment strategy as needed. This habit ensures your financial plan remains aligned with your goals and adapts to any changes in your income or expenses.

Real-life success stories can illustrate the transformative power of financial apps. Consider the case of a young couple who struggled with managing their finances after moving in together. They decided to use YNAB to create a shared budget. By setting financial goals and tracking their spending, they could save enough money for a down payment on their first home within two years. Another example involves a recent college graduate who invested small amounts using Robinhood. By setting up automatic contributions and leveraging the platform's educational resources, he grew his portfolio significantly over a few years, setting a solid foundation for his financial future. These stories highlight how leveraging technology can lead to significant financial improvements and help you achieve your goals more efficiently.

Case Study: Financial Success Through Tech

Meet Alex, a recent graduate who had always found managing money overwhelming. He decided to try out a few financial apps to see if they could help. He started with Credit Karma to monitor his credit score, YNAB for budgeting, and Robinhood for investing. With Credit Karma, Alex received alerts about his score and tips for improvement. YNAB helped him track his spending and save money each month. Robinhood allowed him to start investing small amounts, gradually building his portfolio. Within a year, Alex saw significant improvements in his credit score and accumulated savings and began understanding the basics of investing.

This transformation gave him the confidence to make informed financial decisions and set long-term goals.

As you navigate the complexities of financial management, remember that the right tools can make a world of difference. By selecting apps that align with your needs, integrating them into your daily routine, and staying proactive, you can take control of your finances and build a secure future. These tools simplify financial management and empower you to make informed decisions, achieve goals, and enjoy peace of mind.

SUMMARY

This chapter explored the foundational concepts of financial literacy and independence. We covered budgeting basics, building and maintaining good credit, saving for emergencies, and beginning your investment journey. We also discussed how understanding and managing your financial resources can provide stability and confidence in your financial future.

KEY POINTS:

- Budgeting is Essential: Track income and expenses, set realistic goals, and regularly review your budget.
- Credit Matters: Maintain a good credit score by paying bills on time and avoiding high balances.
- Saving for Emergencies: Build an emergency fund to cover at least 3–6 months of expenses.
- Start Small with Investing: Compound interest grows your wealth, even with small initial investments.

CALL TO ACTION:

- Create a Budget: Use a spreadsheet or app (like Mint or YNAB) to start budgeting your income and expenses this month.
- Reflect on Your Credit: Write down three specific actions you can take to improve or maintain your credit score. Consider setting up automatic payments or scheduling regular credit report checks.

2

CAREER READINESS AND JOB HUNTING

I magine you're scrolling through job listings, and one catches your eye. The description matches your skills perfectly, and the company's values align with yours. Excited, you quickly prepare your resume and cover letter, eager to make a great first impression. But days turn into weeks, and you have yet to hear back. What went wrong?

Imagine the potential impact of a well-crafted resume and cover letter. These documents are not just pieces of paper; they are your introduction to potential employers. They need to capture your attention and convey your qualifications clearly and compellingly. The significance of a well-crafted resume and cover letter cannot be overstated in your job search journey. With the right approach, you can make a great first impression and open doors to exciting opportunities.

A poorly crafted resume often looks cluttered, lacks focus, and fails to highlight critical achievements. It might include irrelevant information or generic phrases that don't add value. For instance, a resume with vague job descriptions like "responsible for various tasks" doesn't tell the employer much about your capabilities. In contrast, a well-crafted resume is concise, well-organized, and highlights specific accomplishments. Instead of saying "responsible for various tasks," a strong resume might say, "Managed a team of five to increase sales by 20% within six months." This specificity provides a clear picture of your abilities and impact.

A compelling cover letter is equally crucial. It serves as a personal introduction and a sales pitch to intrigue recruiters. A well-written cover letter can make your application stand out, demonstrating your enthusiasm for the role and the organization. For example, if you're applying for a marketing position, your cover letter should highlight relevant projects and achievements that align with the job requirements. It should also convey your passion for the field and the company. According to Indeed (2024), a cover letter tailored to the job and includes specific details from the job description can significantly increase your chances of getting noticed.

Creating a standout resume requires attention to detail and a clear structure. Start with a header with your name, contact information, and a professional email address. A professional email address, such as your full name or a variation of it, adds credibility to your application. The following section should be a summary or objective statement briefly outlining your career goals and critical qualifications. This is followed by your work experience, listed in reverse chronological order. For each position, use bullet points to describe your responsibilities and achievements. Focus on action verbs and quantifiable results. Instead of 'worked on marketing campaigns,' say 'developed and executed marketing campaigns that increased web traffic by 30%.' Include relevant skills and certifications in a separate section, and list your education at the end.

Tailoring your resume and cover letter for each job application is essential. Start by analyzing the job description to identify key terms and skills the employer is looking for. Incorporate these keywords into your resume and cover letter to show you're a strong match for the position. For instance, if the job description emphasizes project management skills, highlight your experience in this area with specific examples. Customize your cover letter by addressing it to the hiring manager directly and referencing the company's mission or recent projects. Demonstrating your knowledge of the company and how your skills align with their needs shows genuine interest and effort.

Common mistakes can easily undermine your application. Overloading your resume with the necessary information can make it easier for employers to find the details. Stick to relevant experiences and achievements that align with the job you're applying for. Using generic phrases like "hardworking" or "team player" without providing context can make your resume and cover letter blend in rather than stand out. Instead, use specific examples to illustrate these qualities. For instance, instead of saying you're a 'hardworking team player,' you could say 'I led a team that successfully launched a new product, demonstrating my ability to work collaboratively and under pressure.' ignoring proofreading is another critical error. Typos and grammatical mistakes can make you appear careless. Always review your documents carefully, or ask someone else to proofread them for you.

Reflection Section: Perfecting Your Resume and Cover Letter

Take a moment to review your current resume and cover letter. Identify areas where you can add more details and quantify your achievements. Write down three essential skills or experiences that align with the job you're applying for. For example, if you're applying for a marketing position, you might want to highlight your experience in social media management, content creation, and campaign analysis. Update your documents to highlight these aspects and ensure there are no errors. Reflecting on and refining your resume and cover letter can significantly improve your chances of making a solid first impression with potential employers. Remember, your resume and cover letter are not static documents. They should evolve with your career, so it's essential to keep them updated and tailored to each job application.

Crafting a strong resume and cover letter is the first step towards securing your dream job. Attention to detail, tailoring your documents to each application, and avoiding common mistakes can make a lasting impression on potential employers and increase your chances of landing an interview.

2.1 MASTERING THE JOB INTERVIEW: TIPS AND TRICKS

Preparing for different types of interviews is crucial because each format has unique nuances. In-person interviews are the most traditional, involving multiple stages with other team members. The key here is to make a strong impression right from the handshake. Dress appropriately for the industry to show that you understand the company culture. For example, a suit might be expected in finance, while business casual could be more fitting for tech. Phone screenings are typically the first hurdle. These are usually brief but aim to assess your initial fit for the role. Your tone and clarity become paramount since you can't rely on body language. Have your resume before you, and be ready to discuss your experiences concisely. Virtual interviews have become increasingly common, especially post-pandemic. These require a quiet, well-lit space and a stable internet connection. Ensure your background is professional and free from distractions. Test your equipment beforehand to avoid technical glitches. Being well-prepared for these different interview formats will give you the confidence and readiness to tackle any situation.

Answering common interview questions effectively requires preparation. The STAR method—Situation, Task, Action, Result—is a powerful technique for structuring your responses. For instance, if asked about a time you led a project, describe the context (Situation), your responsibility (Task), the steps you took (Action), and the outcome (Result). Behavioral questions often probe your experiences to predict future performance. Questions like "Tell me about a time you faced a conflict at work" are designed to see how you handle challenges. Prepare several examples that highlight your problem-solving skills, teamwork, and adaptability. The STAR method equips you with a structured approach to answer such questions, making you feel competent and ready. Developing a personal elevator pitch is also crucial. This brief, compelling summary of who you are and what you bring to the table should be practiced until it feels natural. It's your chance to make a memorable first impression, so make it count.

Making a positive impression during an interview goes beyond just answering questions. Your appearance and demeanor play significant roles. Dress appropriately for the industry to show you understand the company's culture. Maintain positive body language—sit up straight, make eye contact, and nod to show engagement. Smiling can convey confidence and friendliness. Asking insightful questions about the company and the role can set you apart. This shows you've done your homework and are genuinely interested in the position. Questions like "Can you describe the team I'd be working with?" or "What are the greatest challenges currently facing the department?" demonstrate curiosity and engagement.

Handling complex interview scenarios can be challenging, but preparation can make a significant difference. Addressing gaps in employment is crucial. Be upfront about the reasons, whether it was due to further education, personal reasons, or job searching, and focus on how you used that time productively. Responding to unexpected questions requires a calm and thoughtful approach. Take a moment to think before you answer, and if you genuinely don't know, it's okay to say so and express a willingness to learn. Managing interview anxiety is another common concern. Practice deep breathing exercises before the interview to calm your nerves. Visualization techniques can also help; imagine yourself succeeding in the interview to build confidence. Remember, interviews are as much about assessing fit for you as they are for the employer, so approach the conversation as a two-way dialogue.

2.2 NETWORKING LIKE A PRO: BUILDING PROFESSIONAL RELATIONSHIPS

Imagine being at a career fair surrounded by potential employers and industry professionals. You're nervous but excited, knowing this is an opportunity to make valuable connections. Networking is crucial in career development. It opens doors to job opportunities through referrals, which can sometimes be more effective than applying online. Referrals often come from trusted sources, making employers more inclined to consider your application. Networking also helps you stay updated on industry trends and best practices. You can learn about the latest technologies, methodologies, and market shifts by talking to professionals in your field. This knowledge can give you a competitive edge. Moreover, networking allows you to gain mentorship and career advice. Experienced professionals can offer guidance, share their experiences, and provide insights you might not get elsewhere.

To build and maintain professional relationships, you need to be proactive. Attending industry events and conferences is a great start. These gatherings provide a platform to meet people who share your interests and career goals. When you attend these events, prepare by researching the attendees and having a few conversation starters ready. Utilizing online platforms like LinkedIn is another effective strategy. LinkedIn allows you to connect with professionals globally, join industry groups, and participate in discussions. Your profile should be updated to reflect your skills and experiences. Engaging in informational interviews can also be beneficial. Reach out to professionals in your field and request a brief meeting to learn about their career paths and seek advice. These interviews provide valuable insights and potentially lead to job opportunities.

Following up and maintaining connections are vital aspects of networking. After meeting someone, send a thank-you note. This simple gesture shows appreciation and keeps you on their radar. Regularly updating your network on your career progress is also essential. Share your achievements, new skills, or any changes in your career path. This keeps your connections informed and engaged. Offering help and value to your connections can strengthen relationships. Share relevant articles, provide your expertise, or introduce them to other professionals. Building a network is a two-way street; giving value to others can make your connections more meaningful.

Networking has challenges, but it can be navigated with the right approach. Overcoming shyness or introversion can be difficult, but practice and preparation can help. Start with smaller events to build confidence, and set small goals like speaking to three new people. Dealing with rejection or unresponsiveness is another common issue. Only some people will respond to your outreach, and that's okay. Keep reaching out and focus on the positive interactions. Managing time spent on networking activities is crucial, especially if you have a busy schedule. Dedicate specific networking times, whether attending events, engaging on LinkedIn, or following up with contacts. This ensures consistency without overwhelming your schedule.

2.3 NAVIGATING THE GIG ECONOMY: FREELANCING AND SIDE HUSTLES

The gig economy represents a shift in how we view work and income. It offers flexibility and control over your schedule, which is particularly appealing if you value freedom in your work life. Instead of adhering to a traditional 9-to-5 job, you can choose projects that interest you and work at times that suit your lifestyle. This flexibility allows for a better work-life balance and can be especially beneficial for parents or students. Additionally, the gig economy provides opportunities for diverse income streams. By taking on multiple gigs, you can diversify your sources of income, reducing the risk associated with relying on a single employer. This approach increases financial stability and opens the door to building a varied skill set. Working on different projects across various industries helps you develop a wide range of skills, making you more versatile and marketable.

Identifying and securing freelancing or side hustle gigs requires a strategic approach. Platforms like Upwork, Fiverr, and TaskRabbit are excellent starting points. These websites connect freelancers with clients looking for specific services, from graphic design and writing to handyman tasks and virtual assistance. Creating a compelling profile on these platforms is crucial. Highlight your skills, showcase your portfolio, and gather positive reviews to attract potential clients. Networking within industry-specific communities can also lead to gig opportunities. Attend local meetups, join online forums, and participate in conferences to connect with others in your field. Leveraging social media to showcase your skills and services is another effective tactic. Use LinkedIn, Instagram, or TikTok to share your work, offer insights, and engage with your audience. This builds your personal brand and makes it easier for potential clients to find you.

Balancing multiple freelance projects can be challenging, but effective time management strategies can help. Start by creating a schedule that allocates specific times for each project. Use tools like Google Calendar or Trello to organize your tasks and deadlines. Setting clear boundaries and expectations with clients is essential to avoid overcommitting. Discuss deadlines, deliverables, and communication preferences upfront to ensure everyone is on the same page. Using project management tools can also help you stay organized. Apps like Asana or Monday.com allow you to track your progress, collaborate with clients, and manage multiple projects simultaneously. These tools can streamline your workflow, making it easier to juggle various gigs without feeling overwhelmed.

Financial stability in the gig economy requires careful planning and management. As a freelancer, you'll need to set aside money for taxes since employers don't withhold them for you. Open a separate savings account and regularly deposit a portion of your earnings to cover your tax obligations. Building a client base to ensure steady income is another crucial step. Focus on delivering high-quality work and maintaining strong relationships with your clients. Repeated business and referrals can provide a consistent flow of projects. Diversifying your income sources is also essential. Don't rely solely on one platform or type of gig. Explore different avenues and services to broaden your opportunities. This approach mitigates risk and ensures that others can pick up the slack if one income stream slows.

For instance, consider a graphic designer who takes on various projects through Upwork, participates in local art fairs, and offers online courses on digital design. By diversifying her income sources, she creates a stable financial foundation while expanding her skills and client base. This strategy enhances financial security and provides a sense of professional fulfillment. Balancing multiple freelance projects and ensuring economic stability in the gig economy is achievable with the right approach and tools. You can thrive in this flexible and dynamic work environment by managing your time effectively, setting clear boundaries, and diversifying your income. The gig economy offers many opportunities for those willing to embrace its challenges and rewards, making it an attractive option for young adults and parents.

2.4 PROFESSIONAL ETIQUETTE: HOW TO CONDUCT YOURSELF AT WORK

Imagine walking into your first day at a new job. You're eager to make a good impression but unsure how to navigate the professional environment. Understanding the basics of professional behavior is crucial. Punctuality is a fundamental aspect. Arriving on time shows reliability and respect for others' schedules. It sets a positive tone and demonstrates that you value your job. Equally important is respectful communication. Whether you're speaking with colleagues or supervisors, maintaining a polite and professional tone fosters a collaborative atmosphere. Please treat everyone with the same level of respect, regardless of their position. Maintaining a positive attitude can also make a significant difference. Approaching tasks with enthusiasm and a can-do mindset boosts your productivity and inspires those around you.

Navigating workplace dynamics requires an understanding of the company culture and values. Every organization has its unique environment, so take the time to observe and learn. Pay attention to how colleagues interact, the norms for communication, and the unspoken rules about office conduct. Building rapport with team members is essential for a harmonious work environment. Take a genuine interest in your colleagues, engage in conversations, and offer help when needed. Small gestures like remembering birthdays or celebrating team successes can strengthen bonds. Managing office politics diplomatically is another critical skill. Avoid getting involved in gossip or negative talk. Instead, focus on building alliances through positive interactions and demonstrating integrity in your actions.

Effective communication is the backbone of professional success. Writing professional emails is a skill that cannot be overstated. Keep emails clear and concise, and always include a relevant subject line. Use proper grammar and punctuation, and avoid slang or overly casual language. Active listening during meetings is equally important. Show your engagement by making eye contact, nodding, and taking notes. Be clear and articulate your points effectively when it's your turn to speak. Delivering constructive feedback can be challenging but is necessary for growth. Focus on the behavior or task, not the person, and offer suggestions for improvement positively. For example, instead of saying, "You did this wrong," try, "I noticed this issue; here's how we can improve."

Handling workplace conflicts professionally is vital. Start by identifying the root cause of the conflict. Is it miscommunication, differing values, or something else? Once you understand the underlying issue, approach it with a problem-solving mindset. Instead of assigning blame, focus on finding a solution for everyone involved. For instance, if two team members have a scheduling conflict, work together to find a compromise that accommodates both parties. If the conflict persists or escalates, seeking mediation might be necessary. An impartial third party, such as a supervisor or HR representative, can help facilitate a resolution. It's essential to address conflicts promptly to prevent them from affecting the work environment.

Your behavior and communication skills are constantly on display in a professional setting. How you conduct yourself can significantly impact your career trajectory. By being punctual, communicating respectfully, and maintaining a positive attitude, you lay the groundwork for strong professional relationships. Understanding and adapting to workplace dynamics help you navigate the complexities of different work environments effectively. Clear and professional communication ensures that your messages are understood and respected. Handling conflicts with a problem-solving approach demonstrates maturity and leadership. These skills are not just about getting the job done; they're about building a reputation as a reliable, respectful, and effective professional.

2.5 NEGOTIATING YOUR SALARY AND BENEFITS

Imagine you've just received a job offer for a position you've been eyeing for months. The excitement is palpable, but there's a crucial step that can influence your career growth significantly: salary negotiation. Negotiating your salary and benefits is not just about securing a higher paycheck; it's about establishing your value as a professional and setting the tone for your future earnings. A higher starting salary means more money in your pocket now and translates into compounded financial benefits over time. For instance, annual raises and bonuses are often calculated as a percentage of your base salary, so starting higher can have a substantial long-term impact. Additionally, negotiating effectively can enhance your job satisfaction, showing that you value your skills and contributions, leading to a more fulfilling work experience.

Preparing for salary negotiations requires thorough research and self-assessment. Start by researching industry salary standards for your role and location. Websites like Glassdoor and PayScale can provide valuable insights into what others in similar positions are earning. This information gives you a solid benchmark and helps you understand what is reasonable to ask for. Next, assess your skills and experiences. Make a list of your accomplishments and contributions in previous roles. Quantify these achievements whenever possible, as numbers can make a compelling case. For example, if you increased sales by 20% or managed a project that saved the company thousands of dollars, these are worth highlighting. Preparing a detailed list of your contributions reinforces your value and provides concrete evidence to support your salary request.

Effective negotiation strategies can make a significant difference in the outcome. One technique is to practice negotiation conversations with a mentor or trusted friend. Role-playing different scenarios can help you feel more confident and prepared. Using objective data to support your requests is another powerful tactic. Presenting industry salary benchmarks and your quantified achievements makes your case more persuasive. Be ready to discuss benefits and perks beyond salary. Sometimes, companies may not be able to meet your salary expectations but can offer other valuable benefits such as additional vacation days, flexible working hours, or professional development opportunities. Being open to negotiating these aspects can result in a more favorable overall compensation package.

Common negotiation pitfalls can undermine your efforts if you're not careful. One major mistake is accepting the first offer without negotiation. Employers often expect candidates to negotiate, and the initial offer usually differs from the maximum they are willing to pay. By accepting the first offer, you might leave money on the table. Another pitfall is undervaluing your skills and experiences. Confidence in your abilities is crucial. Remember, your contributions and expertise have value, and it's important to advocate for yourself. Failing to consider the total compensation package is another common error. Salary is just one part of the equation. Benefits such as health insurance, retirement plans, and work-life balance can significantly impact your overall job satisfaction and financial well-being. Make sure to evaluate the entire package before deciding.

Mastering salary negotiation is about preparation, confidence, and effective communication. By researching industry standards, assessing your skills, and practicing your negotiation strategies, you can confidently approach the conversation and articulate your value clearly. Avoiding common pitfalls and being open to discussing the total compensation package ensures that you make informed decisions that benefit your long-term career growth and satisfaction.

Negotiating your salary and benefits sets the stage for your professional development and financial stability. With the right strategies and mindset, you can confidently navigate this crucial aspect of your career and achieve outcomes that reflect your true worth. Transitioning into the next chapter, we'll explore the broader aspects of health and wellness, ensuring you maintain a balanced and fulfilling life as you advance in your career.

SUMMARY:

In this chapter, you learned how to craft a standout resume and cover letter, prepare for various types of job interviews, and effectively network to increase your job prospects. Each section provides practical strategies for success, from resume-building tips to mastering networking and interview skills. You also explored the growing gig economy and its opportunities, as well as the basics of professional etiquette in the workplace.

KEY POINTS:

- A well-crafted resume and cover letter can significantly impact your job search.
- Interview preparation and understanding common questions are vital to success.
- Networking opens doors to job opportunities and professional growth.
- The gig economy offers flexibility and income diversification for those who want non-traditional work.
- Professional behavior and communication skills are crucial for long-term career success.

CALL TO ACTION:

- Refine Your Resume and Cover Letter: Take immediate steps to update your resume and cover letter based on the chapter's recommendations. Add quantifiable achievements, use action verbs, and tailor your documents to the job description.
- Practice Interview Skills: Set aside time to prepare for common interview questions using the STAR method and develop a concise elevator pitch.

3

HEALTH AND WELLNESS

A few years ago, my friend Mark found himself constantly exhausted and struggling to keep up with his demanding job. Despite working long hours, he felt he was always running on empty. One day, it hit him: his diet was a mess. He was grabbing fast food, skipping meals, and relying on caffeine to get through the day. Mark decided to take control by planning his meals ahead of time. The transformation was incredible. Not only did he start feeling more energetic, but he also saved money and reduced food waste. This chapter is dedicated to helping you achieve the same benefits through effective meal planning and budget-friendly recipes.

3.1 MEAL PLANNING AND BUDGET-FRIENDLY RECIPES

The importance of meal planning extends beyond just having something to eat. It plays a crucial role in maintaining your health and managing your budget. When you plan your meals, you ensure that your diet includes a variety of nutrients necessary for your body's well-being. This reduces the temptation to rely on unhealthy, convenient options. Additionally, meal planning helps in saving money. You can significantly reduce your grocery expenses by buying bulk and planning your meals around sales and seasonal produce. Moreover, it reduces food waste. When you know what you'll eat and when you're less likely to buy unnecessary items that spoil your fridge.

Creating an effective meal plan involves several steps, each designed to make your life easier and healthier. Start by assessing your dietary needs and preferences. Are you trying to eat more vegetables or reduce your sugar intake? Make a list of your nutritional goals and favorite foods. Next, create a shopping list based on your meal plan. This helps you stay focused at the grocery store and avoid impulse buys. Consider batch cooking and meal prepping as well. Set aside a specific day to prepare multiple meals for the week. This saves time and ensures you always have healthy options available. For example, you can cook a big pot of chili or a tray of roasted vegetables used in various dishes throughout the week.

Budget-friendly recipes are essential for maintaining a healthy diet without breaking the bank. Easy one-pot meals like vegetable stir-fries, lentil soups, and pasta dishes are economical and require minimal cleanup. Nutrient-dense salads and soups can be made with affordable ingredients like beans, grains, and seasonal vegetables. For instance, a hearty vegetable soup with kale, sweet potatoes, and chickpeas can be filling and nutritious. Healthy snacks and breakfasts can also be prepared in advance. Overnight oats with fruits and nuts or homemade energy bars are great examples. These recipes help you avoid expensive and unhealthy snack options.

Sticking to a meal plan can be challenging, but several strategies can help you maintain consistency. Keeping a meal journal is a great way to track what you eat and how it makes you feel. This can provide insights into your eating habits and help you adjust as needed. Setting aside time for meal prep is crucial. Dedicate a few hours each week to prepare your meals. This might involve chopping vegetables, cooking grains, and portioning meals for the week. Incorporating leftovers creatively can also keep your meals interesting. For example, leftover roasted chicken can be used in salads, sandwiches, or stir-fries, reducing waste and saving time.

Reflection Section: Your Meal Planning Strategy

Take a moment to think about your current eating habits. Do you often find yourself resorting to takeout or processed foods? Write down three specific dietary goals you want to achieve. These could be eating more vegetables, reducing sugar intake, or cooking more meals at home. Next, outline a basic meal plan for the week that aligns with these goals. Include a shopping list and a designated meal prep day. Reflecting on and planning meals can lead to better health and financial savings.

3.2 FITNESS ON A BUDGET: HOME WORKOUTS AND OUTDOOR ACTIVITIES

Imagine waking up each morning feeling refreshed and energized, ready to tackle the day. Regular exercise can make this a reality, offering numerous physical and mental health benefits. Stay active improves cardiovascular health, reducing the risk of heart disease, high blood pressure, and stroke. Exercise enhances your mood and relieves stress by releasing endorphins, the body's natural mood elevators. You'll find that regular workouts increase your energy levels, making daily tasks feel less daunting and more manageable. These benefits collectively contribute to a healthier, happier life.

Home workout routines are a convenient and cost-effective way to stay fit. You don't need expensive gym memberships or fancy equipment to get a good workout. Bodyweight exercises like push-ups, squats, and lunges are perfect for building strength and endurance. These exercises can be modified to suit any fitness level, making them accessible to everyone. Resistance band routines offer another versatile option. Bands are inexpensive and portable, allowing you to perform various exercises that target different muscle groups. Incorporating yoga and stretching exercises into your routine can improve flexibility, balance, and mental clarity. Yoga practices, such as Sun Salutations or basic stretching exercises, can be done in the comfort of your home with minimal equipment.

Outdoor activities provide an excellent opportunity to stay active while enjoying nature. Running or jogging in local parks is a great way to boost cardiovascular health and clear your mind. Parks often have dedicated running paths, offering a safe and scenic route for your workouts. Hiking trails and nature walks are another fantastic option. These activities not only provide a good workout but also allow you to connect with nature, which can be incredibly calming and rejuvenating. Many communities offer sports and recreation programs that are either free or low-cost. Joining a local soccer league or participating in a community yoga class can help you stay active and meet new people, making your fitness journey more enjoyable.

Staying motivated to exercise regularly can be challenging, but several strategies can help you maintain consistency. Setting fitness goals and tracking your progress is a powerful motivator. Whether your goal is to run a 5K, increase your strength, or stay active, having a clear target gives you something to work towards. Use a fitness journal or app to track your workouts and celebrate your achievements. Finding a workout buddy or joining a fitness group can also motivate you. Exercising with others provides accountability and makes the experience more enjoyable. Fitness apps like Strava or Nike Training Club offer guided workouts and progress tracking, helping you stay on course and mix up your routine.

Exercise Tracking Sheet to help you stay on track:

- Consider using an exercise tracking sheet.
- Create a simple table with columns for the date, type of workout, duration, and any notes.
- Fill it in after each workout to monitor your progress and identify patterns.

For example, you might feel more energized after morning workouts or prefer certain exercise types. This insight can help you tailor your routine to better suit your needs and preferences. Keeping a record of your workouts enables you to stay accountable and provides a sense of accomplishment as you see your progress over time.

Staying fit doesn't have to be expensive or time-consuming. With a mix of home workouts, outdoor activities, and a few motivational strategies, you can maintain a regular fitness routine that supports your physical and mental well-being.

3.3 UNDERSTANDING MENTAL HEALTH: RECOGNIZING AND MANAGING STRESS

Consider for a moment the feeling of being overwhelmed by everyday tasks. You might notice a constant headache or find yourself snapping at loved ones over minor issues. These are not just passing annoyances; they are signs of stress and anxiety affecting your mental health. Mental health is as crucial as physical health because it impacts your overall well-being and quality of life. When your mental health is compromised, it affects your physical health, too. Stress can lead to conditions such as high blood pressure, weakened immune response, and even heart disease. Maintaining good mental health is essential for a balanced and healthy life.

Recognizing the signs of stress and anxiety is the first step toward managing them. Physical symptoms can be varied and sometimes subtle. You might experience headaches, unexplained fatigue, or muscle tension. These symptoms are your body's way of signaling that something is off. Emotionally, stress can manifest as irritability, anxiety, or feelings of sadness. You might be more prone to anger or tears without an apparent reason. Behavioral changes are also common. You might notice changes in your sleep patterns, such as insomnia or sleeping too much. Your appetite might shift, leading to overeating or undereating. Awareness of these signs helps you identify when stress is taking a toll on your mental health.

Managing stress effectively involves practical strategies to incorporate into your daily routine. Mindfulness and meditation practices are excellent tools for reducing stress. Mindfulness involves paying attention to the present moment without judgment. It can be as simple as taking a few minutes each day to focus on your breathing or noticing the sensations in your body. Meditation practices, such as guided meditation or progressive muscle relaxation, can help calm your mind and reduce anxiety. Deep breathing exercises are another effective technique. When you feel overwhelmed, take a few deep breaths, inhaling slowly through your nose and exhaling through your mouth. This simple act can help lower your heart rate and promote a sense of calm. Journaling and expressive writing allow you to process your thoughts and emotions. Writing about your experiences can provide clarity and help you understand your stressors better.

There are numerous resources available for mental health support if you find that self-help strategies are not enough. Counseling and therapy options provide professional guidance to help you navigate your mental health challenges. Speaking with a licensed therapist can offer personalized strategies and a safe space to explore your feelings. Mental health hotlines and online resources are also valuable. Organizations like the National Alliance on Mental Illness (NAMI) offer helplines and online support for those in need. Support groups and community services provide a sense of connection and shared experience. Joining a support group allows you to share your struggles with others who understand, offering mutual support and encouragement.

Maintaining good mental health requires ongoing effort and a willingness to seek help when needed. By recognizing the signs of stress, incorporating stress management techniques, and utilizing available resources, you can take proactive steps to support your mental well-being.

3.4 BUILDING A SELF-CARE ROUTINE: PRIORITIZING YOUR WELL-BEING

Understanding self-care and its importance is crucial for maintaining overall health. Self-care involves taking deliberate actions to care for your physical, mental, and emotional well-being. It's about pampering yourself and preventing burnout, enhancing emotional resilience, and promoting a balanced lifestyle. When you prioritize self-care, you equip yourself to handle life's challenges more effectively. It helps you recharge and remain productive, ensuring you can meet your responsibilities without feeling overwhelmed.

Creating a personalized self-care routine starts with identifying activities that resonate with you. Think about what makes you feel relaxed and rejuvenated. It might be reading a book, walking in nature, or engaging in a creative hobby like painting. Once you've identified these activities, schedule regular self-care time. Blocking out specific times in your calendar for these activities ensures they become a priority rather than an afterthought. Balancing self-care with daily responsibilities is also essential. It's easy to push self-care aside when you're busy, but making it a non-negotiable part of your routine can help maintain your well-being.

Examples of self-care practices vary widely, allowing you to choose what best fits your needs and preferences. Engaging in hobbies and creative pursuits can provide a mental break from daily stressors and stimulate your mind in new ways. Practicing gratitude and positivity exercises, such as keeping a gratitude journal, can shift your focus to the positive aspects of your life, enhancing your overall outlook. Taking breaks and resting when needed is another vital aspect of self-care. Listening to your body and permitting yourself to sleep can prevent burnout and improve your productivity in the long run.

Maintaining a consistent self-care routine can be challenging, but several strategies can help. Setting reminders and alarms can prompt you to take breaks and engage in self-care activities. Reflecting on the benefits of self-care can also motivate you to keep it up. Notice how you feel after taking time for yourself, and use that positive reinforcement to maintain your routine. Adjusting the routine as needed ensures it remains relevant and practical. Your needs may change over time, so be flexible and willing to adapt your self-care activities accordingly.

Self-Care Reflection Exercise

Take a moment to list three self-care activities that make you feel relaxed and happy. Next, look at your weekly schedule and identify times you can consistently fit these activities. Write these times down and set reminders on your phone or calendar. Reflect on how these activities make you feel and adjust your routine to ensure it continues serving you well.

Self-care is not a luxury but necessary for a balanced and healthy life. By understanding its importance, creating a personalized routine, and maintaining it consistently, you can prevent burnout, enhance emotional resilience, and lead a more fulfilling life.

3.5 SLEEP HYGIENE: TIPS FOR BETTER SLEEP

Imagine waking up every morning feeling refreshed, focused, and ready to tackle the day. Quality sleep plays a crucial role in achieving this. It impacts your overall well-being in numerous ways. Sleep is essential for cognitive function and memory. During sleep, your brain processes and consolidates information from the day, making it easier to recall facts and figures. A lack of sleep can impair your ability to think, problem-solve, and make decisions. Physically, sleep allows your body to repair and rejuvenate. It plays a vital role in muscle recovery, immune function, and overall physical health. You're more susceptible to illnesses and injuries when you don't sleep enough. Additionally, sleep has a significant influence on your mood and mental health. Proper rest can help stabilize your emotions, reduce stress, and improve your overall outlook on life.

Creating a sleep-friendly environment is the first step towards better sleep. Start by maintaining a comfortable room temperature. The ideal sleeping temperature is typically between 60-67 degrees Fahrenheit. Keeping your bedroom cool can help you fall asleep faster and longer. Minimizing noise and light disruptions is also crucial. Use blackout curtains to block out external light, and consider using a white noise machine or earplugs to drown out disturbing sounds. Investing in a good mattress and pillows can significantly affect your sleep quality. A mattress supporting your body and pillows that align your neck can prevent discomfort and promote deeper sleep.

Establishing a bedtime routine can signal your body that it's time to wind down. Setting a regular sleep schedule is essential. Try to go to bed and wake up simultaneously every day, even on weekends. This consistency helps regulate your body's internal clock, making it easier to fall asleep and wake up naturally. Practicing relaxation techniques before bed can also prepare your mind and body for sleep. Activities like reading a book, taking a warm bath, or practicing gentle yoga can help you relax. Avoiding screens and stimulating activities before bed is crucial. The blue light emitted by phones, tablets, and computers can interfere with your body's production of melatonin, a hormone that regulates sleep. Try to turn off electronic devices at least an hour before bedtime.

Addressing common sleep issues can help you improve your sleep quality. Managing insomnia and sleep anxiety involves creating a calming bedtime routine and avoiding caffeine and heavy meals before bed. Techniques such as progressive muscle relaxation or guided imagery can help relax your body and mind. If you struggle with sleep apnea or other disorders, consult a healthcare professional for proper diagnosis and treatment. Simple lifestyle changes, such as maintaining a healthy weight and sleeping on your side, can alleviate some symptoms. Improving sleep quality through diet and exercise is also effective. A balanced diet of fruits, vegetables, and whole grains can promote better sleep. Regular physical activity can help you fall asleep faster and enjoy deeper sleep, but avoid vigorous exercise close to bedtime.

Understanding and implementing good sleep hygiene can transform your nights and days. By prioritizing sleep, optimizing your sleep environment, and addressing any issues, you can enjoy the benefits of better rest.

3.6 NAVIGATING HEALTHCARE: UNDERSTANDING INSURANCE AND FINDING DOCTORS

When I first got my health insurance, I remember needing clarification on the jargon and options. It felt like a foreign language. Understanding the basics of health insurance is crucial for managing your healthcare needs effectively and avoiding unexpected medical bills. Health insurance comes in various forms, primarily HMOs (Health Maintenance Organizations) and PPOs (Preferred Provider Organizations). HMOs typically require you to choose a primary care physician (PCP) and get referrals to specialists, which can help coordinate your care but may limit your choices. PPOs offer more flexibility, allowing you to see any healthcare provider without a referral, but usually at a higher cost.

You understand how premiums, deductibles, and co-pays work, which is essential. The premium is the amount you pay monthly for your insurance plan. The deductible is the out-of-pocket amount before your insurance starts covering expenses. After meeting your deductible, co-pays are fixed amounts you pay for specific services, like doctor visits or prescriptions. Understanding these terms helps you budget for medical expenses and choose the right plan. Preventive care, which includes services like vaccinations and screenings, is often covered at no cost under most plans. Preventive care can help catch health issues early, saving money and improving overall health.

Choosing the right health insurance plan involves comparing various options to find the best fit for your needs and budget. Start by evaluating your personal health needs. Do you have any chronic conditions requiring regular treatment? Are you planning to start a family soon? These factors can influence the type of coverage you need. Next, consider your budget. Look at the premium costs, but also factor in the deductible and copays. A lower premium might seem attractive, but you could pay more out-of-pocket if the deductible is high. Evaluate the coverage for specific services you might need, such as mental health care, physical therapy, or prescription drugs. Ensure the plan you choose covers these services adequately.

Finding and choosing healthcare providers is another critical aspect of navigating healthcare. Start by researching providers within your insurance network to avoid higher out-of-pocket costs. Online reviews and ratings can provide insights into a doctor's reputation and patient experiences. Scheduling and preparing for appointments is essential. Make a list of questions and concerns beforehand to ensure you cover everything during your visit. Building a relationship with your healthcare provider is beneficial. A good relationship with your doctor can lead to better care and more personalized advice. Feel free to switch providers if your current one isn't meeting your needs.

Making the most of healthcare resources involves effectively understanding and utilizing your health benefits. Familiarize yourself with your plan, including preventive services, specialist visits, and emergency care. Accessing telehealth and virtual care options can be convenient and cost-effective. Many insurance plans now cover virtual visits, allowing you to consult with health-care providers from home. This is particularly useful for minor ailments or follow-up appointments. Seeking second opinions is also a valuable resource. If you're faced with a significant medical decision or diagnosis, getting a second opinion can provide additional perspectives and ensure you make informed choices about your health.

Navigating healthcare can be manageable. You can confidently take control of your health by understanding health insurance basics, choosing the right plan, finding the best providers, and making the most of your healthcare resources. This ensures you receive the care you need and helps you manage your healthcare costs effectively.

Maintaining your health and wellness is a continuous process. The skills and knowledge you gain here will serve you well as you navigate the complexities of adulthood. Next, we will explore how to build a strong foundation in financial literacy, empowering you to manage your money effectively and achieve your financial goals.

SUMMARY

This chapter explored the fundamental components of maintaining health and wellness. Effective meal planning can enhance your nutrition and save money, while home workouts and outdoor activities provide budget-friendly fitness options. Understanding stress and its management is essential for mental health, and building a consistent self-care routine can prevent burnout. Lastly, developing good sleep hygiene and navigating healthcare systems ensures you prioritize your physical and psychological well-being.

KEY POINTS

- Meal Planning: Reduces food waste, saves money, and promotes better nutrition.

- Fitness on a Budget: Bodyweight exercises, resistance bands, and outdoor activities can provide effective, low-cost fitness options.
- Mental Health: Managing stress is crucial for overall well-being and can be achieved through mindfulness, deep breathing, and journaling.
- Self-Care: Regular self-care prevents burnout and improves emotional resilience.
- Sleep Hygiene: Good sleep habits improve cognitive function, mood, and physical health.

CALL TO ACTION

- Meal Planning & Recipes: Create a simple meal plan for the upcoming week using budget-friendly recipes that align with your dietary goals.
- Fitness on a Budget: Choose one home workout or outdoor activity to incorporate into your weekly routine.
- Mental Health Awareness: Spend five minutes practicing mindfulness or deep breathing exercises to manage stress.
- Self-Care Routine: Schedule three self-care activities into your weekly calendar.

4

EMOTIONAL INTELLIGENCE AND RELATIONSHIPS

One story stands out vividly when I think back to my college days. I had a roommate named James, who was brilliant but often misunderstood. His sharp mind and quick wit were undeniable, but he struggled to communicate his thoughts and emotions. This led to numerous conflicts with friends and professors. One night, after another argument, he confided in me about his frustration. It wasn't that he didn't care; he didn't know how to express himself without causing misunderstandings. This chapter is dedicated to helping you avoid James's plight by mastering the art of effective communication.

4.1 EFFECTIVE COMMUNICATION: SPEAKING AND LISTENING SKILLS

Effective communication is the cornerstone of all successful personal or professional relationships. Strong communication skills allow you to convey your thoughts and feelings, ensuring your understanding. This not only fosters deeper connections but also prevents conflicts from arising. In a professional setting, articulating ideas and listening to others can enhance collaboration and productivity. Imagine working on a group project where everyone can share their perspectives openly and respectfully. This kind of environment leads to innovative solutions and a harmonious workplace. On a personal level, effective communication strengthens bonds with family and friends, creating a supportive network where everyone feels heard and valued.

Active listening is a crucial component of effective communication. It involves entirely focusing on the speaker, understanding their message, and responding thoughtfully. One technique to improve your listening skills is maintaining eye contact. This shows the speaker that you are engaged and interested in their words. Nodding and using verbal affirmations like "I see" or "Go on" can encourage the speaker to continue and feel validated. Avoiding interruptions and distractions is also essential. When someone is speaking, resist the urge to check your phone or think about your response. Instead, concentrate on their words and the emotions behind them. This level of attentiveness fosters a deeper connection and mutual respect.

Improving your speaking skills is equally important. Start by using "I" statements to express your feelings and needs. For example, instead of saying, "You never listen to me," try, "I feel unheard when we don't discuss things." This approach reduces defensiveness and opens the door for constructive dialogue. Keeping your messages concise and to the point helps avoid misunderstandings. Rambling or over-explaining can dilute your message and confuse the listener. Checking for understanding by asking questions is another effective technique. After sharing your thoughts, you might say, "Does that make sense?" or "How do you feel about that?" This ensures that both parties are on the same page and clarifies potential misinterpretations.

Non-verbal communication plays a significant role in how your message is received. Recognizing and interpreting body language can provide insights into the speaker's feelings. For instance, crossed arms might indicate defensiveness, while leaning in can show interest. A furrowed brow might indicate confusion or disagreement, while a smile can convey agreement or understanding. Using gestures and facial expressions effectively can also enhance your message. A warm smile or a nod can express empathy and understanding, while a firm handshake can establish confidence and trust. It's essential to be aware of cultural differences in non-verbal communication. In some cultures, direct eye contact is seen as respectful; in others, it might be considered aggressive. Understanding these nuances can help you navigate conversations more smoothly and avoid unintentional offense. Reflection Section: Practicing Effective Communication

Take a moment to reflect on a recent conversation that didn't go as planned. What could you have done differently to improve the outcome? Write down three strategies you can implement next time, such as maintaining eye contact, using "I" statements, or checking for understanding. These techniques can help you communicate more effectively and strengthen your relationships.

Effective communication is more than just exchanging information; it's about understanding the emotions and intentions behind the words. You can build stronger, more meaningful relationships by honing your speaking and listening skills and paying attention to nonverbal cues.

4.2 CONFLICT RESOLUTION: TECHNIQUES FOR RESOLVING DISPUTES

Understanding the nature of conflict is fundamental to resolving it effectively. Conflicts arise for various reasons, often stemming from miscommunication or differing values. For instance, you might disagree with a friend because you interpreted their words differently than they intended. Differing values can also lead to conflicts, such as when two people have opposing views on important issues like politics or parenting styles. When conflicts are left unresolved, they can have adverse effects on relationships. Resentment builds, trust erodes, and communication breaks down. These unresolved tensions can create a toxic environment, making maintaining healthy, supportive relationships complex.

Conflict resolution strategies are not just about finding a solution; they're about fostering understanding and empathy. When you actively listen, you're not just hearing the words; you're engaging with the speaker and showing that you value their perspective. On the other hand, empathy involves more than just understanding their feelings and viewpoints; it's about genuinely putting yourself in their shoes. Finding common ground is another effective strategy. By focusing on what you agree on rather than the points of contention, you can create a foundation for a more productive discussion. Compromise and negotiation are also essential. Sometimes, you must give a little to reach a mutually acceptable solution. Negotiation involves discussing options and finding a middle ground where both parties feel satisfied. By approaching conflict resolution with empathy and understanding, you can navigate disputes constructively and strengthen your relationships. Handling conflicts constructively involves a step-by-step approach. Start by identifying the root cause of the conflict. Ask yourself what the underlying issue is and why it has caused tension. Once you understand the problem, express your concerns without blame. Use "I" statements to share how you feel and why. For example, say, "I feel hurt when plans are changed at the last minute" instead of "You always cancel on me." This reduces defensiveness and opens the door for open communication. Collaborate on finding a solution. Work together to brainstorm ideas and agree on a way forward. This collaborative approach ensures that both parties feel heard and valued.

Managing emotions during conflicts is not just a good practice; it's a vital skill that can keep discussions productive and relationships intact. When emotions run high, it's easy to say things you don't mean or escalate the situation. Taking breaks to cool down can prevent this. Step away for a few minutes to collect your thoughts if you feel overwhelmed. Practicing deep breathing exercises can also help. Inhale deeply through your nose, hold for a few seconds, and exhale slowly through your mouth. This simple technique can calm your mind and reduce stress. Visualization can be another effective calming technique. Picture a peaceful scene or imagine a positive outcome for the conflict. This can shift your mindset and help you approach the situation more clearly. By managing your emotions during disputes, you can stay calm and in control, ensuring that your discussions and relationships remain productive. Imagine a scenario where you're having a heated argument with a sibling over household chores. Both of you feel frustrated and unheard. Instead of shouting, take a break to cool down. When you return, practice active listening. Let your sibling share their perspective without interruption. Acknowledge their feelings and express your own using "I" statements. Collaborate on a solution, such as creating a chore schedule that works for both of you. This approach resolves the conflict and strengthens your relationship by fostering mutual respect and understanding.

Conflict Resolution Exercise

Think about a recent conflict you experienced. Reflect on your steps and identify areas where you could have applied these strategies. Write down the root cause of the conflict, how you expressed your concerns, and the solution you reached. Consider how managing your emotions differently impacts the outcome. This exercise can help you build better conflict resolution skills for future disputes.

Understanding the nature of conflict, employing effective resolution strategies, and managing emotions are vital to resolving disputes constructively. By approaching conflicts with empathy, open communication, and a willingness to compromise, you can transform disagreements into opportunities for growth and stronger relationships.

4.3 BUILDING HEALTHY FRIENDSHIPS: QUALITY OVER QUANTITY

I met so many people in college that my social circle felt endless. However, when I faced a challenging situation, only a few friends stood by me. This experience taught me that having a few strong friendships is far more beneficial than maintaining many superficial ones. Quality friendships provide emotional support and trust, creating a safe space to share your deepest fears and greatest joys. These relationships positively impact your mental health, offering a sense of belonging and reducing feelings of loneliness and anxiety. Knowing someone genuinely cares for you and has your back can be incredibly comforting.

Healthy friendships are defined by certain traits that make them supportive and fulfilling. Mutual respect and understanding are foundational. You respect each other's boundaries, opinions, and choices, even when they differ from your own. Reciprocity and balance in the relationship are also crucial. Both friends should contribute equally, whether it's through emotional support, time spent together, or sharing responsibilities. One-sided friendships, where only one person is giving, can lead to resentment and burnout. Honest and open communication is another critical characteristic. Speaking your mind without fear of judgment fosters a deeper connection and helps resolve misunderstandings promptly.

Regular check-ins and time together are essential to nurture and maintain these valuable friendships. Life gets busy, but making time for your friends shows you value the relationship. Consistent interaction strengthens the bond, whether a weekly phone call or a monthly coffee date. Being supportive during tough times is another crucial aspect. Showing up for your friends when they need you the most strengthens the relationship and builds trust. Celebrate each other's successes, no matter how small. Whether a promotion at work or mastering a new hobby, acknowledging and celebrating these moments brings joy and positivity into your friendship.

Identifying and addressing toxic friendships is vital for your well-being. Signs of poisonous behavior include manipulation, constant negativity, and a lack of support. If you have a friend who always puts you down, makes you feel guilty, or drains your energy, it's time to reassess the relationship. Setting boundaries with toxic friends is the first step. Communicate your limits and what behaviors you will not tolerate. If they continue disrespecting your boundaries, consider ending the friendship. Knowing when to end a friendship is challenging but necessary for mental and emotional health. Letting go of relationships that no longer serve you or bring you happiness is okay.

Imagine you have a friend who constantly criticizes your decisions and makes you feel inferior. You've tried talking to them, but nothing changes. To protect your well-being, you set clear boundaries, such as limiting your time together and avoiding topics that trigger negativity. Over time, if the toxic behavior persists, you might choose to end the friendship. Though difficult, this decision can lead to personal growth and open space for healthier relationships.

Building and maintaining healthy friendships requires effort and intentionality. By focusing on quality over quantity, nurturing supportive traits, and addressing toxicity when necessary, you can cultivate friendships that enrich your life and contribute to your overall well-being. In the following subchapter, we will explore the dynamics of romantic relationships and how to navigate love and commitment effectively.

4.4 ROMANTIC RELATIONSHIPS: NAVIGATING LOVE AND COMMITMENT

Building a robust romantic relationship starts with a foundation of trust and honesty. Trust is the bedrock upon which all other relationship aspects are built. Without it, doubts and insecurities can creep in, eroding the bond between partners. Honesty goes hand in hand with trust. Being truthful about your feelings, intentions, and actions fosters an environment where both partners feel safe and valued. Mutual respect and equality are equally important. Everyone should feel valued and heard, and decisions should be made together, respecting each other's opinions and desires. Effective communication ties all these elements together. Sharing your thoughts openly and listening to your partner with empathy creates a deeper understanding and connection.

Intimacy in a relationship, both emotional and physical, requires ongoing effort. Regularly expressing affection and appreciation can make your partner feel loved and valued. This could be simple gestures like holding hands, leaving a sweet note, or verbally expressing gratitude. Spending quality time together is another critical component. Whether it's a weekly date night or a shared hobby, these moments help strengthen your bond. Being open about your needs and desires is crucial for maintaining intimacy. Talk about what makes you feel loved and what you need from your partner. This openness fosters a deeper connection and ensures both partners feel satisfied and understood.

Challenges are inevitable in any romantic relationship, but how you handle them can determine the relationship's strength. Dealing with jealousy and insecurity involves open communication and reassurance. Talk about your feelings and work together to build trust. Navigating differences in values and goals requires compromise and understanding. For example, if one partner values career advancement while the other prioritizes family time, finding a balance that respects both perspectives is essential. Managing long-distance relationships brings its own set of challenges. Consistent communication and setting clear expectations can help bridge the physical gap. Plan visits and create shared experiences even when apart to maintain the connection.

Commitment and future planning are vital aspects of a robust romantic relationship. Setting shared goals and visions gives your relationship a direction and purpose. Please discuss what you want to achieve together, whether it's buying a home, traveling, or starting a family. These shared goals can strengthen your bond and provide motivation. Discussing important life decisions, such as marriage and children, ensures you're on the same page and can plan accordingly. Supporting each other's personal growth is also crucial. Encourage your partner to pursue their passions and goals and celebrate their achievements. This support fosters a sense of partnership and mutual respect.

Imagine a couple who regularly set aside time to discuss their future. They discuss their dreams, make plans, and support each other's aspirations. This ongoing dialogue not only keeps them aligned but also strengthens their commitment. They navigate challenges by openly discussing their feelings and finding solutions together. When one partner feels insecure, the other provides reassurance, reinforcing their trust. They prioritize quality time, whether it's a weekend getaway or a simple dinner at home, ensuring they stay connected. They build a resilient and fulfilling relationship by fostering intimacy, handling challenges with care, and planning their future together.

Relationships require effort, understanding, and a willingness to grow together. By focusing on trust, intimacy, and mutual support, you can navigate the complexities of love and commitment, creating a partnership that stands the test of time. Each moment spent nurturing your relationship is an investment in a future filled with shared joy and mutual respect.

4.5 PROFESSIONAL RELATIONSHIPS: BUILDING RAPPORT WITH COLLEAGUES

Establishing strong workplace relationships can be a game-changer for your career. These relationships not only enhance your job satisfaction but also boost your productivity. You create a supportive and collaborative environment when you get along well with your colleagues. This positive atmosphere can make your workday more enjoyable and less stressful. A harmonious work environment encourages teamwork and innovation, leading to higher-quality work and better results. Imagine working where everyone supports each other and contributes to a common goal. Such an environment can significantly enhance your overall well-being and career success.

Building rapport with colleagues requires genuine effort and interest. Start by showing a sincere interest in their lives. Ask about their weekend plans, hobbies, or how their family is doing. This shows that you care about them as individuals, not just as coworkers. Help and support, when needed, is another excellent way to build strong relationships. Whether assisting with a challenging project or covering for someone who needs to leave early, these small acts of kindness can go a long way. Engaging in team-building activities can also strengthen your bond with colleagues. Participating in group outings, office potlucks, or even virtual team games can help you connect on a personal level, making it easier to work together professionally.

Maintaining professionalism while being friendly is a balancing act. Setting boundaries is essential to ensure your friendliness doesn't compromise your professionalism. Be approachable and open, but also know when to draw the line. Avoid engaging in office gossip or harmful behavior, damaging your reputation and trustworthiness. Demonstrating reliability and integrity is crucial. Always follow through on your commitments and be honest in your interactions. This builds trust and respect among your colleagues, establishing you as a dependable and credible professional.

Workplace conflicts are inevitable, but handling them professionally can make a significant difference—approach conflicts with a problem-solving attitude. Find a solution for everyone instead of focusing on who's at fault. This proactive approach can defuse tension and foster a more collaborative environment. If the conflict escalates and cannot be resolved between the parties involved, seeking mediation from supervisors or HR can be beneficial. They can provide an impartial perspective and help facilitate a resolution. Focus on solutions rather than blame. Highlight the issue at hand and discuss ways to address it constructively.

Imagine a situation where you and a colleague disagree on how to approach a project. Instead of letting the disagreement fester, take the initiative to discuss it openly. Express your perspective and listen to theirs. Find common ground and brainstorm possible solutions together. If the conflict persists, involve your supervisor to mediate and provide guidance. Focusing on solutions and maintaining a professional demeanor can resolve the dispute amicably and strengthen your working relationship.

Building strong professional relationships involves:

- Showing genuine interest in your colleagues.
- Offering support.
- Engaging in team-building activities.

Balancing friendliness with professionalism is critical to maintaining a positive work environment. A problem-solving approach ensures that conflicts are resolved constructively, fostering a collaborative and supportive workplace. Professional relationships contribute significantly to career success, job satisfaction, and overall well-being, making them an essential aspect of professional life.

4.6 SETTING BOUNDARIES: PROTECTING YOUR MENTAL AND EMOTIONAL HEALTH

When I started working full-time, I constantly said yes to every request, whether a new project at work or helping a friend move on the weekend. It didn't take long for me to feel overwhelmed and burnt out. This experience taught me the importance of setting boundaries for my mental and emotional well-being. Boundaries act as safeguards, preventing burnout and stress by ensuring you don't overextend yourself. They help maintain healthy relationships by clearly defining what is acceptable and what is not. Without boundaries, you might feel resentful, exhausted, and undervalued.

Identifying personal boundaries requires self-reflection and awareness. Reflecting on past experiences can provide insights into what makes you uncomfortable or stressed. Think about moments when you felt taken advantage of or overwhelmed. These instances can highlight areas where boundaries are needed. Assessing your comfort levels in various situations is also essential. Pay attention to your feelings and physical responses in different scenarios. If something feels off, it signals that a boundary might be necessary. Communicating boundaries is the next step. Use straightforward language to express your limits. For example, you might say, "I need some time for myself and can't take on extra work this weekend."

Setting and enforcing boundaries can be challenging, but there are practical strategies to help. Using assertive communication is critical. Assertiveness involves expressing your needs and limits confidently and respectfully. It's about standing up for yourself without being aggressive. Saying no without guilt is another crucial aspect. Understand that it's okay to prioritize your well-being. When you decline a request, you're not being selfish; you're taking care of yourself. Being consistent in enforcing boundaries is vital. Once you set a limit, stick to it. Consistency can lead to clarity and make it easier for others to respect your boundaries.

Dealing with boundary violations requires a calm and direct approach. Address the issue as soon as it occurs. Calmly explain how the violation made you feel and reiterate your boundary. For example, "I felt disrespected when you didn't consider my time. I need you to respect my schedule." If boundaries are repeatedly ignored, it's essential to re-evaluate the relationship. Consider whether the relationship is worth maintaining if it continually undermines your well-being. Seeking support from trusted friends or professionals can also be beneficial. Talking to someone who understands your situation can provide validation and guidance. A therapist or counselor can offer strategies to strengthen boundaries and handle violations effectively.

Imagine you have a friend who constantly asks for favors but never reciprocates. You've tried setting boundaries, but they continue to overstep. Addressing the issue calmly, you might say, "I've noticed that I'm often helping out, but it's not reciprocated. I need a more balanced relationship where we both support each other." If the behavior persists, consider whether this friendship is healthy for you. Seeking advice from a trusted friend or therapist can help you navigate this decision and provide support.

Setting boundaries is not just about protecting your time and energy; it's about respecting yourself and ensuring that others do. You can create a healthier, more balanced life by identifying your limits, communicating them clearly, and enforcing them consistently. Boundaries help you maintain mental and emotional well-being, fostering respectful and supportive relationships.

Each chapter of this book builds on the last, equipping you with the tools to navigate adulthood confidently. As we move forward, we'll delve into practical life skills that empower you to thrive in every aspect of your life.

SUMMARY:

This chapter emphasized the importance of emotional intelligence in personal and professional relationships. Key aspects include effective communication, conflict resolution, building healthy friendships, maintaining romantic relationships, fostering professional connections, and setting boundaries to protect mental and emotional well-being. By applying these principles, readers can build stronger, healthier relationships and improve their emotional intelligence.

KEY POINTS:

- Emotional intelligence is critical for forming meaningful relationships.
- Effective communication, both verbal and non-verbal, strengthens bonds.
- Conflicts are inevitable but can be resolved through empathy and understanding.
- Healthy friendships prioritize quality over quantity.
- Romantic, solid relationships are built on trust, respect, and open communication.
- Professional relationships benefit from genuine connection and collaboration.
- Setting boundaries is essential to maintain mental and emotional well-being.

CALL TO ACTION:

At the end of each section, actively reflect on your experiences and apply the strategies mentioned.

Example: Reflect on a recent conversation that didn't go well. Write down three strategies you could have used to improve the outcome.

Effective Communication Tools:

Active listening techniques (e.g., maintaining eye contact, nodding, verbal affirmations).

Using "I" statements (e.g., "I feel hurt when...").

- Conflict Resolution Techniques:

Break conflicts down into root causes.

Steps to managing emotional escalation: deep breathing, stepping away for a short break.

- Building Healthy Friendships:

Traits of a supportive friendship: mutual respect, balance, and reciprocity.

Identify toxic friendships and set boundaries.

- Romantic Relationships:

Building trust and intimacy involves consistent communication and emotional and physical closeness.

- Professional Relationships:

Networking techniques and rapport-building strategies (e.g., engaging in team-building activities).

BOOK REVIEW REQUEST

"The best way to find yourself is to lose yourself in the service of others."

— MAHATMA GANDHI.

I Need Your Help!

Hello! If you've found this book helpful in learning the "Essential Life Skills for Young Adults," I would love to hear your thoughts. Your review can help others discover how to take control of their journey as well, just like you have! By sharing your experience, you're not just helping me—you're helping future readers who are ready to start their own "Life Skills" adventures.

Writing a review is quick and easy. A few sentences about what you enjoyed most or how the book has helped you can make a big difference. Your words could inspire someone else to take that first step toward financial freedom. So, thank you for being part of this journey with me!

5

PRACTICAL LIFE SKILLS

One evening, I received a frantic call from my younger cousin, Jake. He had just moved into his first apartment and discovered water pooling under his kitchen sink. Panicked, he didn't know what to do. I guided him through tightening a loose pipe, and he managed to stop the leak. This incident made me realize how vital basic home maintenance skills are. Knowing how to handle minor repairs can save you money, prevent damage, and give you a sense of independence. This chapter, which is directly relevant to your daily life, will equip you with essential home maintenance skills to keep your living space safe and functional.

5.1 BASIC HOME MAINTENANCE: DIY REPAIRS AND UPKEEP

Regular home maintenance is crucial for both safety and cost savings. Paying attention to minor issues can lead to significant problems down the line. For instance, if left unattended, a minor water leak can cause extensive water damage, mold growth, and even structural issues. Regular upkeep prevents hazards like fire risks from faulty wiring or clogged dryer vents. Additionally, maintaining your home increases the longevity of appliances and structural elements, saving you from costly replacements and repairs. For example, routinely cleaning your HVAC filters ensures efficient operation and extends the system's lifespan.

Common household repairs can initially seem daunting, but you can handle many yourself with some knowledge and the right tools. Fixing a leaky faucet, for instance, often involves replacing a worn-out washer or cartridge. Start by turning off the water supply, then disassemble the faucet to access the worn parts. Replace them with new ones, reassemble the faucet, and turn the water back on. Unclogging drains is another common task. A plunger or a drain snake can usually clear minor clogs. For more stubborn blockages, a mixture of baking soda and vinegar followed by hot water can help dissolve the buildup. Repairing drywall holes is straightforward as well. Clean the area, apply a patch, and use joint compound to smooth it out before sanding and painting. Replacing a broken light fixture involves:

- Turning off the power at the breaker.
- Disconnecting the old fixture.
- Connecting the new one.
- Securing it in place.

Having the right tools on hand makes home maintenance tasks much more accessible. A hammer and a set of screwdrivers (both flathead and Phillips) are essential for various repairs. Pliers and wrenches are crucial for plumbing tasks and tightening bolts. A utility knife is handy for cutting materials like drywall, while a tape measure ensures accurate measurements for any project. A power drill is invaluable for drilling holes and driving screws quickly and efficiently. Each tool serves multiple purposes, making them versatile additions to your toolkit.

Preventive maintenance is about staying ahead of potential issues. Changing HVAC filters regularly keeps your heating and cooling systems running efficiently, reducing energy costs and preventing breakdowns. Inspecting smoke detectors is a simple yet vital task. Test them monthly and replace batteries at least once a year. Cleaning gutters ensures proper water drainage and prevents damage to your roof and foundation. It's best to do this in the spring and fall when leaves and debris are most likely to accumulate. Checking for pest infestations is another crucial preventive measure. Look for signs like droppings, chewed materials, or nests, and address any issues promptly to avoid larger infestations.

Home Maintenance Checklist

1. Monthly Tasks:
   - Test smoke detectors and carbon monoxide detectors.
   - Check HVAC filters and replace if dirty.
   - Inspect plumbing for leaks.
2. Seasonal Tasks:
   - Clean gutters in spring and fall.
   - Inspect the roof for damage or wear.
   - Check for pest infestations and take preventive measures.
3. Annual Tasks:
   - Service your HVAC system.
   - Inspect and clean dryer vents.
   - Check the exterior of your home for signs of wear and damage.

Regular home maintenance not only keeps your living space safe and functional but also eventually saves you money. By learning these basic skills and staying proactive with preventive measures, you can handle minor issues before they become major problems. This not only gives you peace of mind but also empowers you to take control of your living environment, knowing that you have the skills to address any issues that may arise.

CALL TO ACTION:

- Action 1: Create and follow a basic home maintenance schedule (monthly, seasonal, annual).
- Action 2: Start a toolkit with essential tools like screwdrivers, a hammer, and pliers, and plan to expand it over time.
  - Tools: Basic toolkit essentials include a hammer, pliers, screwdrivers (both flathead and Phillips), a utility knife, a tape measure, and a power drill.

5.2 CAR MAINTENANCE 101: ESSENTIAL TIPS FOR CAR OWNERS

Imagine driving to an important event, and suddenly, your car starts making strange noises. You pull over, feeling a mix of anxiety and frustration. Regular car maintenance could have prevented this scenario. Keeping your vehicle in good shape enhances its performance and prevents costly repairs. By taking responsibility for your car's maintenance, you can ensure it runs smoothly and keeps you safe on the road.

Changing the oil is one of the most critical maintenance tasks. Start by parking your car on a level surface and placing a drain pan under the oil pan. Use a wrench to remove the drain plug and let the old oil drain out completely. Once drained, replace the drain plug and remove the old oil filter. Install a new filter, ensuring it is snug but not over-tightened. Finally, refill the engine with the recommended amount and type of oil using a funnel to avoid spills. This process keeps the engine lubricated, preventing over-heating and damage.

Replacing air filters is another simple yet vital task. Over time, air filters get clogged with dirt and debris, reducing airflow to the engine and decreasing performance. To change the air filter, locate the filter housing near the engine. Open the housing, remove the old filter, and replace it with a new one. This ensures your engine gets clean air, improving fuel efficiency and performance.

Checking tire pressure and tread is essential for safe driving. Underinflated tires can cause poor handling and increased fuel consumption, while worn-out treads can reduce traction, especially in wet conditions. Use a tire pressure gauge to check the pressure of each tire, comparing it to the recommended levels in your car's manual. Use a penny to check the tread depth. Insert the penny into the tread with Lincoln's head facing down. If you can see the top of his head, it's time to replace the tires. Keeping your tires in good condition ensures better handling and safety.

Replacing windshield wipers is a simple task that significantly improves visibility during adverse weather conditions. Lift the wiper arm away from the windshield and press the trim tab to release the old wiper blade. Attach the new blade by clicking it into place. Test the wipers to ensure they're working correctly. This quick fix ensures clear visibility in rain or snow, enhancing your safety on the road.

Spotting early warning signs of car problems can save you from more significant issues and expenses. Unusual noises or vibrations often indicate a problem. Squealing brakes may mean the brake pads need replacing, while a vibrating steering wheel could signal alignment issues. Pay attention to the warning lights on your dashboard. The check engine light, for example, can indicate various issues, from a loose gas cap to more serious engine problems. Addressing these warnings promptly can prevent further damage. Fluid leaks under the car are another red flag. Puddles of oil, coolant, or transmission fluid can signify leaks that need immediate attention.

Having essential tools in your car can help you tackle minor issues on the go. A tire pressure gauge is crucial for regular tire checks, ensuring they're inflated correctly. A socket and wrench set are versatile for various tasks, from tightening bolts to changing the oil. A car jack and jack stands are necessary to lift the car safely when changing tires or undercarriage inspections. Jumper cables are vital for unexpected battery issues, allowing you to jump-start your car if the battery dies.

Car Maintenance Checklist

1. Monthly Checks:
   ◦ Inspect oil and coolant levels.
   ◦ Check tire pressure and tread depth.
   ◦ Ensure headlights, turn signals, and brake lights are functioning.
2. Every 3 Months or 3,000-5,000 Miles:
   ◦ Change the oil and oil filter.
   ◦ Rotate tires to ensure even wear.
   ◦ Wax the vehicle every six months to protect the paint.
3. Long-Term Checks:
   ◦ Inspect transmission fluid and change as needed.
   ◦ Check shocks and struts every 50,000 miles.

○ Flush and refill the coolant system based on manufacturer recommendations.

Regular maintenance keeps your car running smoothly and safely, reducing the risk of breakdowns and extending its lifespan. By learning these basic tasks and staying vigilant for warning signs, you can ensure your vehicle remains reliable and efficient.

5.3 RENTING YOUR FIRST APARTMENT: WHAT TO LOOK FOR AND HOW TO SECURE IT

Finding your first apartment is an exciting yet daunting task. Start by researching potential apartments using online rental platforms like Zillow and Apartments.com. These websites allow you to filter properties based on various criteria, such as price range, number of bedrooms, and amenities. Location is crucial, so consider proximity to your work or school. A shorter commute can save you time and reduce transportation costs.

Additionally, assess the neighborhood's safety and amenities. Look for nearby grocery stores, parks, and public transportation options. Online reviews and local crime reports can provide valuable insights into the area's safety.

Once you've found a few potential apartments, you'll need to understand the rental application process. This typically involves preparing necessary documents like your ID, proof of income, and sometimes a credit report. Landlords want to ensure you can afford the rent, so having your pay stubs or bank statements ready is essential. Writing a rental application letter can set you apart from other applicants. Briefly introduce yourself, explain why you're interested in the apartment, and highlight your reliability as a tenant. Providing references from previous landlords or employers can also strengthen your application. They can vouch for your responsibility and reliability, increasing your chances of securing the apartment.

When viewing apartments, it's vital to inspect several key factors. Check for signs of damage or pests, such as water stains on ceilings or droppings in corners. These can indicate underlying issues that might cause problems later. Assess the water pressure and plumbing by turning on faucets and flushing toilets. Weak water pressure or slow drainage can signal plumbing problems. Evaluate the natural light and ventilation in each room. Good natural light can make a space feel larger and more inviting, while proper ventilation is crucial for maintaining a healthy living environment. Remember to test light switches and electrical outlets to ensure they function correctly.

Negotiating lease terms can feel intimidating, but it's an essential step in securing a favorable rental agreement. Start by discussing the rental price and lease duration with the landlord. You can negotiate a lower monthly rent if you're signing a longer lease. It's also worth asking for repairs or improvements before moving in. For example, if you notice worn-out carpeting or outdated appliances, request replacements or updates as part of the lease agreement. Understanding the terms of the lease is crucial. Ensure you know what's included in the rent, such as utilities or parking, and clarify any policies on subletting, pets, or lease renewal. These details can impact your overall living experience and financial commitments.

Moving into your first apartment is a significant milestone, marking a step towards independence and responsibility. By thoroughly researching potential apartments, preparing a solid application, carefully inspecting properties, and negotiating favorable lease terms, you can find a place that meets your needs and fits your budget. This process helps you secure suitable living space and builds valuable skills for managing future rentals and housing decisions.

Call to Action:

- Action 1: Research rental properties using websites like Zillow or Apartments.com and create a list of potential apartments.
- Action 2: Prepare the necessary documents (ID, proof of income, references) to streamline your rental application process.

5.4 UNDERSTANDING LEGAL DOCUMENTS: CONTRACTS, LEASES, AND MORE

When I first signed a lease for my apartment, I felt a mix of excitement and anxiety. The stack of papers in front of me seemed overwhelming. Understanding legal documents can be daunting, but it's crucial for protecting your interests. Legal agreements share standard components that you should be familiar with:

1. Identify the parties involved. These individuals or entities entering the contract, such as you and your landlord.
2. Pay close attention to the terms and conditions. This section outlines each party's obligations, including payment schedules, the duration of the agreement, and specific responsibilities.
3. Ensure that all signatures and dates are present.

These validate the contract and indicate that all parties agree to the terms.

Reading and understanding contracts requires a careful approach. Start by identifying essential clauses. These critical elements define the agreement, such as payment terms, termination conditions, and penalties for breach. Recognizing red flags and unfavorable terms is also vital. Look out for clauses that seem one-sided or impose excessive penalties. For example, a clause that allows the landlord to enter your apartment without notice can be problematic. Knowing when to seek legal advice is crucial. Consult a lawyer if you encounter complex language or terms you need help understanding. This can prevent future disputes and ensure you fully comprehend your obligations and rights.

Young adults often encounter various legal documents. Employment contracts are standard when starting a new job. These documents outline your role, salary, benefits, and termination conditions. Understanding these terms helps you know what to expect and ensures you're treated fairly. Rental agreements are essential for anyone renting an apartment. They detail the terms of your lease, including rent, duration, and maintenance responsibilities. Service contracts, such as those for utilities or internet services, specify the terms of service, payment schedules, and cancellation policies. Reading these carefully helps you avoid unexpected charges and ensures you know how to terminate the agreement if needed.

Safeguarding against legal issues involves some practical steps. Always keep copies of all signed documents. These can be invaluable if disputes arise. For instance, having a copy of your lease can help resolve conflicts with your landlord. Documenting communications with landlords or employers is another good practice. Keep records of emails, letters, and notes from phone calls. This creates a paper trail that can support your case if disagreements occur. Knowing your rights and responsibilities is fundamental. Familiarize yourself with local tenant laws, employment rights, and consumer protection regulations. This knowledge empowers you to advocate for yourself and seek redress if your rights are violated.

Understanding legal documents is a critical life skill. It ensures you are informed and protected in various situations, from renting an apartment to starting a new job. By familiarizing yourself with the essential components of contracts, learning how to read and interpret them, and knowing the types of documents you might encounter, you can confidently navigate these agreements. Taking steps to safeguard against legal issues further enhances your ability to manage your affairs responsibly and effectively.

5.5 GROCERY SHOPPING ON A BUDGET: TIPS AND TRICKS

Planning your grocery shopping trip is crucial in saving money and time. Creating a shopping list based on your meal plans for the week can ensure you buy only what you need, reducing the temptation to make impulse purchases. Start by setting a grocery budget that aligns with your financial goals. Allocating a specific amount for groceries each week helps you stay within your means. Checking weekly store flyers for sales and discounts can also significantly cut costs. Many stores offer digital flyers, making comparing prices and planning your shopping trip easy. This preparation helps avoid overspending and ensures you get the best deals.

When you arrive at the grocery store, several strategies can help you save money. Buying in bulk for non-perishable items like rice, pasta, and canned goods can offer substantial savings over time. These items have a long shelf life, so stocking up during sales makes sense. Choosing store brands over name brands is another effective way to reduce your grocery bill without sacrificing quality. Store brands are often produced by the same manufacturers as name brands but are sold at a lower price. Using coupons and loyalty programs can also add up to significant savings. Many stores offer digital coupons to load onto your loyalty card or app. Be sure to check for these before heading out to maximize your discounts.

Selecting nutritious and budget-friendly foods is possible with some smart choices. Prioritizing fresh produce in season ensures you get the best prices and quality. Seasonal fruits and vegetables are often cheaper and more flavorful. Buying frozen vegetables and fruits is a great alternative when fresh produce is unavailable or too expensive. They are usually frozen at peak ripeness, retaining their nutritional value and taste. Opting for whole grains and legumes provides essential nutrients and is cost-effective. Items like brown rice, quinoa, lentils, and beans are versatile and can be used in various dishes, making them a staple in budget-friendly meal planning.

Avoiding common grocery shopping pitfalls can further enhance your budget-conscious efforts. Shopping when hungry is a significant trap. When you're hungry, everything looks appealing, and you're more likely to buy items you don't need. Eating a snack before shopping can help you stick to your list. Impulse buying is another budget buster. Stores are designed to tempt you with attractive displays and promotions. Staying focused on your list and resisting these temptations is critical. Ignoring unit prices for cost comparisons is a common mistake. Usually displayed on the shelf tag, unit prices help you determine the cost per ounce or pound, making it easier to compare products and choose the best value. For example, a more extensive package might seem more expensive initially, but its unit price could be lowered, offering better value for your money.

Incorporating these strategies into your grocery shopping routine can significantly reduce your monthly expenses. Planning, sticking to your budget, and making informed choices at the store are all steps that contribute to more efficient and cost-effective shopping. These practices help you save money and ensure a well-stocked pantry with healthy and versatile ingredients. By being mindful of your shopping habits and avoiding common pitfalls, you can make the most of your grocery budget and enjoy nutritious meals without breaking the bank.

Call to Action:

- Create a Weekly Grocery Budget: Before your next shopping trip, set a specific budget based on your financial goals and meal plan. Stick to this amount for your next few trips.
- Plan Your Meals: Use this week's store flyers to plan meals and create a shopping list based on items on sale.

5.6 BASIC SEWING AND CLOTHING CARE: EXTENDING THE LIFE OF YOUR WARDROBE

Knowing how to perform simple sewing tasks is like having a hidden superpower. It's not just about saving money on clothing repairs, though that's a significant benefit. Imagine not having to throw away your favorite shirt just because it has a small tear. With basic sewing skills, you can fix it yourself in no time. This saves you money and reduces waste, contributing to a more sustainable lifestyle.

Additionally, sewing allows you to customize and upcycle old clothes. You can turn outdated pieces into trendy outfits, giving your wardrobe a fresh look without spending a fortune. For instance, transforming a pair of old jeans into stylish shorts or adding decorative patches to a plain jacket can breathe new life into your clothes.

Let's start with hemming pants and skirts. This is one of the most common alterations you'll need. Begin by measuring the desired length and marking it with pins. Fold the fabric at the mark and press it with an iron to create a crease. Make tiny, even stitches along the fold using a sewing needle and thread to secure the hem. This technique works for both pants and skirts, ensuring they fit perfectly. Sewing on buttons is another essential skill. Thread a needle and knot the end. Position the button over the existing holes or marks on the fabric. Push the needle through the fabric and button, then back down through the fabric, repeating several times to secure the button. Finish by knotting the thread on the underside. Repairing small tears or holes is straightforward. Start by trimming any loose threads around the tear. Turn the fabric inside out and use a needle and thread to make tiny stitches along the edges of the tear, pulling them together. For larger holes, you might need a patch. Creating simple alterations, like taking in a seam or adjusting a waistband, can also make your clothes fit better. Pin the fabric where you need the adjustment, then sew along the new line, ensuring the stitches are even and secure.

Proper clothing care extends the lifespan of your garments, keeping them looking new longer. Always read and follow care labels to avoid damaging delicate fabrics or colors. For example, some items may require handwashing or dry cleaning only. Proper washing and drying techniques are crucial. Use a gentle cycle for delicate items and cold water to prevent shrinking and color fading. Avoid overloading the washing machine, as this can cause wear and tear. When drying, consider air-drying clothes prone to shrinking or losing shape. Storing seasonal clothing correctly prevents damage and keeps them fresh for when you need them again. Fold and store sweaters and other heavy items in a cool, dry place to avoid stretching. Use garment bags for delicate or special-occasion outfits to protect them from dust and pests.

Having the right tools and supplies for sewing and clothing care makes the process much easier. Start with a basic set of needles and thread. Choose various needle sizes and colors of thread to match different fabrics. Scissors are essential for cutting fabric and trimming threads. A seam ripper is invaluable for removing stitches without damaging the fabric. Measuring tape is crucial for taking accurate measurements before making alterations. Pins are used to hold fabric in place while you sew. Fabric glue and patches are handy for quick repairs or adding decorative elements. Fabric glue can fix small tears without sewing, while patches can cover larger holes or add a personal touch to your clothing.

Reflection Section: Your Sewing Kit Essentials

Take inventory of your current sewing supplies. Do you have the basics: needles, thread, scissors, seam ripper, measuring tape, pins, fabric glue, and patches? If not, list what you need to complete your sewing kit. Having these essentials on hand ensures you're prepared for any clothing repair or alteration that comes your way.

By mastering basic sewing skills and proper clothing care, you can extend the life of your wardrobe and save money. These skills empower you to handle minor repairs, create custom pieces, and maintain your clothes in top condition. Next, we will delve into time management and productivity, exploring balancing work, school, and personal life effectively.

Call to Action:

- Practice Sewing a Button: Grab an old shirt and practice sewing a button following the step-by-step guide in this chapter.
- Take Care of Your Clothes: Review care labels on your clothes and adjust your laundry routine accordingly.

6

TIME MANAGEMENT AND PRODUCTIVITY

I magine waking up one morning, overwhelmed with a long list of tasks and no clear plan. You rush through your day, constantly playing catch-up, and realize you've accomplished little by bedtime. This chaotic cycle can be exhausting and unproductive. Now, consider a different scenario: you wake up knowing exactly what needs to be done and when. Each task has a designated time slot, and you move through your day purposefully and efficiently. This stark contrast illustrates the power of effective time management.

6.1 CREATING A DAILY SCHEDULE: PRIORITIZING TASKS AND ACTIVITIES

A structured daily schedule is not just a list of activities; it's a powerful tool that can significantly boost your productivity and reduce stress. Just look at successful individuals like Oprah Winfrey and Elon Musk, who credit their daily routines for their achievements. Oprah starts her day with meditation and exercise, ensuring she's mentally and physically prepared. Elon Musk, on the other hand, blocks his day in five-minute intervals, maximizing his efficiency. This structured approach to the day can be a game-changer for your productivity and peace of mind.

The benefits of a routine are manifold:

1. It increases focus. When you know what to expect, you can direct your energy towards the task rather than figure out what to do next.
2. Allocating specific time slots for each task improves time management. You can ensure that essential activities are addressed.

Having a plan means you spend less time worrying about what needs to be done and more time doing it. This relief from uncertainty can significantly reduce stress and bring a sense of order and calm to your life.

Creating an effective daily schedule involves a few key steps. Start by listing all your daily tasks and responsibilities. This includes work or school assignments, household chores, and personal commitments. Once you have your list, prioritize tasks based on urgency and importance. Use the Eisenhower Matrix, a tool that helps you categorize tasks into four quadrants: urgent and important, important but not urgent, urgent but not necessary, and neither urgent nor essential. This enables you to focus on what truly matters.

Next, allocate specific time slots for each activity. Use a planner or digital calendar to block out time for each task. For example, set aside morning hours for high-priority work tasks when you're most alert. Reserve afternoons for meetings or collaborative work and evenings for personal time or chores. Be realistic about how long each task will take, and avoid overloading your schedule.

Time-blocking is a powerful technique to enhance productivity. It involves setting dedicated blocks of time for focused work. During these blocks, concentrate on a single task without interruptions. For instance, dedicate 9 AM to 11 AM for writing a report, and resist the urge to check emails or social media during this period. Scheduling breaks is equally important to prevent burnout. Short breaks between time blocks can refresh your mind and maintain energy levels throughout the day. Color-coding different types of tasks can also help you visualize your schedule better. Use one color for work-related tasks, another for personal activities, and a third for breaks. This visual distinction makes it easier to manage your time effectively.

While a structured schedule is beneficial, maintaining flexibility is crucial for adapting to changes and unexpected events. Life is unpredictable, and rigid schedules can lead to frustration. Building buffer time into your schedule to account for delays or unforeseen tasks can help you stay on track even if things don't go as planned, making you feel more adaptable and less stressed.

Another crucial aspect of flexibility in time management is the ability to adjust priorities as needed. If a new urgent task arises, reassess your schedule and shift less critical functions to later. This dynamic approach ensures that you remain in control without feeling overwhelmed. Strategies for handling disruptions include having a backup plan for necessary tasks. If a meeting is canceled, use that time to tackle a pending task or take a break to recharge. This way, disruptions become opportunities rather than setbacks, and you can maintain a sense of order and calm in your daily life.

Maintaining a well-organized schedule requires consistent effort and adaptability. You can create a balanced and productive routine by listing daily tasks, prioritizing them, and using time-blocking techniques. Remember to build flexibility to accommodate the unexpected, ensuring your schedule serves you, not vice versa. This approach enhances productivity and brings a sense of order and calm to your daily life.

6.2 GOAL SETTING: SHORT-TERM AND LONG-TERM PLANNING

Setting goals is like plotting a map for your life. Without clear goals, you might drift aimlessly, unsure which direction to take. Goals provide direction and motivation, acting as a guiding light that helps you navigate through personal and professional growth. Achieving these goals can give you a profound sense of empowerment and control over your life.

Goals also serve as a metric for measuring progress and success. By setting specific targets, you can track your achievements and see how far you've come. This boosts your confidence and helps you identify areas for improvement. The sense of accomplishment that comes from reaching these milestones can be incredibly motivating and rewarding.

Practical goal setting involves using proven frameworks and methods. One popular approach is the SMART criteria: Specific, Measurable, Achievable, Relevant, and Time-bound. This method ensures that your goals are clear and attainable. For example, instead of setting a vague goal like "get fit," a SMART goal would be "run a 5K in under 30 minutes within three months." Another practical framework is OKRs (Objectives and Key Results), often used in professional settings. This involves setting an ambitious objective and defining key results to measure progress. Vision boards and goal journals are also powerful tools. Creating a visual representation of your goals or regularly documenting your progress can keep you motivated and focused.

Creating a goal-setting plan starts with identifying your long-term aspirations. Think about where you want to be in five, ten, or even twenty years. These could be career milestones, personal achievements, or lifestyle changes. Once you have a clear vision of your long-term goals, break them into manageable short-term tasks. For instance, if your long-term goal is to become a published author, your short-term tasks include writing a certain number of words daily, attending writing workshops, and submitting work to publishers. Regularly reviewing and adjusting your goals is crucial. Life is dynamic, and your goals must evolve based on new circumstances or insights. Schedule periodic check-ins to assess your progress and make necessary adjustments.

Obstacles are inevitable when working towards your goals, but overcoming them is part of the process. Staying motivated through challenges requires resilience and a positive mindset. Remind yourself why you set the goal in the first place and visualize the benefits of achieving it. Seeking support from mentors or accountability partners can also be incredibly helpful. Having someone to share your journey with can provide encouragement, advice, and a different perspective on overcoming hurdles. Celebrating small wins along the way is another effective strategy. Acknowledging and rewarding your progress, no matter how minor, keeps you motivated and reinforces your commitment to your goals.

Incorporating these techniques and strategies into your routine can transform your goal-setting approach. By setting clear, actionable goals and breaking them down into manageable tasks, you create a structured path to success. Regularly reviewing and adjusting your goals ensures they remain relevant and attainable while overcoming obstacles with resilience and support keeps you on track. This structured approach enhances productivity and brings a sense of accomplishment and direction to your life.

6.3 OVERCOMING PROCRASTINATION: TECHNIQUES TO STAY FOCUSED

Procrastination is a common issue that many young adults and parents face. Understanding its root causes is the first step to overcoming it. Often, procrastination stems from a fear of failure or perfectionism. You might delay starting a task because you're afraid it won't meet your high standards, or you might worry about criticism. This fear can paralyze you, making it challenging to begin. Another reason people procrastinate is a need for more motivation or interest. Tasks that seem mundane or unengaging can easily be pushed aside for more enjoyable activities. When you don't feel passionate about what you're doing, it's easy to find excuses to avoid it. Feeling overwhelmed by the sheer magnitude of a task can also lead to procrastination. When a project seems too large or complex, breaking it down into manageable steps can feel daunting, causing you to put it off indefinitely.

Practical strategies can make a significant difference in combating procrastination. One effective method is breaking tasks into smaller, manageable steps. Instead of focusing on the entire project, concentrate on completing one small part at a time. This approach makes the task seem less intimidating and gives you a sense of accomplishment as you complete each step. Another technique is the Pomodoro Technique, which involves working in focused intervals, typically 25 minutes, followed by a short break. This method helps maintain high levels of concentration and reduces the mental fatigue that can lead to procrastination. Setting deadlines and creating a sense of urgency can also be motivating. Even if the task doesn't have an immediate deadline, setting one for yourself can provide the push you need to get started and stay on track.

Creating a productive environment is crucial for minimizing distractions and maintaining focus. Start by organizing your workspace. A clutter-free area can help you concentrate better and reduce the temptation to procrastinate. Keep only the essentials on your desk and store away any items that aren't immediately needed. Eliminating digital distractions is also vital. Social media and notifications can quickly derail your focus. Consider using apps like Cold Turkey or StayFocusd to block distracting websites during work hours. Noise-cancelling headphones or background music can further enhance your concentration. Creating a tranquil and orderly workspace can significantly improve your ability to stay focused and productive.

Maintaining focus and accountability requires consistent effort and the right tools. Productivity apps such as Todoist or Trello can help you keep track of tasks and deadlines, ensuring that nothing falls through the cracks. These tools allow you to create to-do lists, set reminders, and monitor your progress. Finding an account-ability partner can also be incredibly beneficial. Sharing your goals and progress with someone else provides external motivation and support. This person can offer encouragement and constructive feedback and hold you accountable for meeting your deadlines. Rewarding yourself for completing tasks is another effective strat-egy. Small rewards, like taking a short break, enjoying a favorite snack, or spending time on a hobby, can make the process more enjoyable and motivate you to stay on track.

6.4 USING TECHNOLOGY TO BOOST PRODUCTIVITY: APPS AND TOOLS

In today's fast-paced world, technology offers many tools to enhance productivity. Task management apps like Todoist and Trello help you organize your tasks and projects efficiently.

Todoist allows you to create to-do lists, set priorities, and track your progress, making managing personal and professional tasks easier. Trello uses boards, lists, and cards to help you visualize your projects and collaborate with others. These tools streamline your workflow and keep you focused on your goals.

Calendar and scheduling tools like Google Calendar are indispensable for managing your time effectively. Google Calendar lets you schedule events, set reminders, and visualize your entire day, week, or month at a glance. You can sync it across all your devices, ensuring you never miss an appointment or deadline. Note-taking apps such as Evernote and OneNote are also handy. Evernote allows you to capture and organize notes, photos, and web clippings in one place. On the other hand, OneNote offers a digital notebook where you can create separate notebooks, sections, and pages for different projects or subjects. These apps help you keep all your information organized and easily accessible.

Choosing the right productivity apps for your needs involves considering several factors. First, look at the user interface and ease of use. An app with a complicated or cluttered interface can be more of a hindrance than a help. Opt for apps that are intuitive and easy to navigate. Integration with other tools and platforms is another crucial factor. For example, if you use Google Calendar for scheduling, choosing task management apps that sync with it is beneficial. Customizability and features are also important. Some apps offer more features than others, such as tagging, filtering, and advanced search capabilities. Evaluate your most essential features and choose an app that meets those needs.

Integrating technology into your daily routine can significantly boost your productivity. Start by syncing apps across all your devices. This ensures that you can access your tasks, schedules, and notes no matter where you are. Setting reminders and notifications helps you stay on track and remember important tasks or appointments. For example, you can set a reminder in Google Calendar for an upcoming meeting and get a notification on your phone, tablet, and computer. Regularly updating and reviewing your task lists is also crucial. Take a few minutes daily to check off completed tasks, add new ones, and adjust priorities as needed. This keeps your to-do list current and manageable.

Real-life examples can illustrate the transformative power of productivity apps. Consider the case of Lisa, a marketing manager who struggled to keep track of her numerous projects and deadlines. She started using Trello to organize her tasks and collaborate with her team. By creating boards for each project and using lists and cards to break down tasks, Lisa could visualize her work and prioritize effectively. This improved her time management and increased her team's efficiency. Another example is Tom, a college student who used Evernote to take notes during lectures and organize his study materials. By syncing Evernote across his devices, Tom could access his notes anytime, anywhere, making his study sessions more productive and efficient.

Case studies of improved time management and increased focus through technology underscore the benefits. For instance, a freelance graphic designer, Sarah, used Todoist to manage her client projects. By setting priorities and due dates for each task, she could ensure timely delivery and maintain high client satisfaction. Testimonials from individuals who have benefited from productivity apps reveal common themes: enhanced organization, better time management, and reduced stress. These tools help you stay on top of your tasks and provide a sense of control and accomplishment.

Incorporating productivity-enhancing technologies into your routine can transform how you work and manage your time. By selecting the right tools, integrating them effectively, and regularly updating your task lists, you can boost your productivity and achieve your goals more quickly and efficiently.

6.5 BALANCING WORK, SCHOOL, AND SOCIAL LIFE

Balancing work, school, and social life is crucial for overall well-being. When you juggle multiple responsibilities, you quickly feel overwhelmed and stressed. However, finding a balance can prevent burnout and reduce stress significantly. You can maintain your mental and physical health by allocating time for each aspect of your life. Enhancing relationships and social connections is another critical benefit. When you make time for friends and family, you build a support network that can help you through tough times. Moreover, balancing different aspects of your life can improve your academic and work performance. When you're not constantly stressed, you can focus better and be more productive in your tasks.

Managing multiple responsibilities requires practical strategies. Prioritizing tasks is the first step. Identify what needs immediate attention and what can wait. Setting boundaries is equally important. Learn to say no to additional commitments that can overload your schedule. Using time management techniques like time-blocking can also help. Allocate specific times for studying, work, and social activities. This way, you ensure that each area gets the attention it deserves. Seeking support from family and friends can make a big difference. Feel free to ask for help when you need it. Whether it's babysitting, tutoring, or just lending a listening ear, support from loved ones can ease your burden.

Maintaining a healthy work-life balance involves scheduling time for relaxation and hobbies. It's essential to take breaks and engage in activities you enjoy. This could be anything from reading a book to going for a walk. Practicing self-care and mindfulness can also help. Taking care of your mental and physical health should be a priority. Engage in activities that relax and rejuvenate you, like meditation or exercise. Setting realistic goals and expectations is crucial. Understand that you can't do everything all at once. Set achievable targets, and be kind to yourself if you don't meet them. This approach helps you stay motivated and reduces the risk of burnout.

Handling conflicting demands and deadlines is a common challenge. Effective communication with employers and professors is vital. Let them know if you need help to meet a deadline and see if it's possible to negotiate it. Most people are understanding if you communicate your needs clearly and early. Creating contingency plans for busy periods can also be helpful. Identify times when your workload will be heavier and plan accordingly. This might mean doing extra work in advance or scheduling fewer social activities during these times. Preparing for busy periods reduces stress and helps you manage your responsibilities more effectively.

Balancing work, school, and social life is an ongoing process. It requires constant adjustments and a proactive approach. You can effectively manage multiple responsibilities by prioritizing tasks, setting boundaries, and seeking support. Scheduling time for relaxation and hobbies, practicing self-care, and setting realistic goals can help you maintain a healthy balance. Remember, asking for help and making adjustments as needed is okay. Balancing different aspects of your life is critical to overall well-being and success.

6.6 MINDFULNESS AND MEDITATION: ENHANCING FOCUS AND REDUCING STRESS

Mindfulness is about being fully present in the moment and aware of your thoughts, feelings, and surroundings without judgment. This practice can significantly enhance mental clarity and concentration, allowing you to focus better on tasks. When you're mindful, you become more aware of distractions and can gently steer your attention back to what matters. This heightened focus can improve your productivity and the quality of your work. Additionally, mindfulness promotes emotional regulation. Being present, you can better understand and manage your emotions, leading to fewer impulsive reactions and more thoughtful responses. This emotional stability can strengthen your relationships and overall well-being.

Incorporating mindfulness into daily life doesn't require drastic changes. Simple practices can make a big difference. Mindful breathing exercises are a great starting point. Take a few minutes to focus on your breath, inhaling deeply through your nose and exhaling slowly through your mouth. Pay attention to the sensation of the air entering and leaving your body. This practice can calm your mind and reduce stress. Body scan meditation is another technique. Lie or sit comfortably and slowly direct your attention to different body parts, starting from your toes and moving up to your head. Notice any sensations, tension, or discomfort without trying to change anything. This practice helps you agree more with your body and releases physical tension. Mindful walking or movement practices involve paying attention to the sensations of movement. Whether walking, stretching, or doing yoga, focus on how your body feels with each movement. This practice can ground you in the present moment and enhance your physical awareness.

Creating a consistent meditation routine can further amplify the benefits of mindfulness. Start by setting aside dedicated time for meditation each day. It doesn't have to be long; even five to ten minutes can be effective. Choose a time when you're least likely to be interrupted, such as early morning or before bed. Find a quiet and comfortable space to sit or lie down without distractions. Your environment plays a significant role in your ability to focus. Guided meditation apps like Headspace or Calm can be beneficial for beginners. These apps offer guided sessions catering to different needs, such as stress reduction, focus, or sleep. Following a guided session can provide structure and support, making it easier to develop a regular practice.

Mindfulness can also be integrated into your daily activities, enhancing your overall experience. Practicing mindful eating involves paying full attention to the process of eating. Notice the colors, smells, textures, and flavors of your food. Eat slowly, savoring each bite, and listen to your body's hunger and fullness cues. This practice can strengthen your relationship with food and enhance your enjoyment of meals. Engaging in mindful listening during conversations means giving the speaker your full attention without planning your response while they're talking. Focus on their words, tone, and body language. This practice can elevate your communication skills and deepen your connections with others. Incorporating mindfulness into work or study breaks can also boost your productivity. Take a few minutes to step away from your tasks, close your eyes, and focus on your breath. This short break can refresh your mind and improve your concentration when you return to work.

As you incorporate these mindfulness practices into your life, you likely notice a ripple effect on your overall well-being. Enhanced focus, reduced stress, and better emotional regulation can improve various aspects of your life, from work performance to personal relationships. Being present in each moment allows you to navigate life's challenges more efficiently and resiliently. These practices don't require significant time or effort, but their impact can be profound, helping you lead a more balanced and fulfilling life.

Maintaining a mindful approach to life can transform your daily experiences, making you more aware, focused, and emotionally balanced. These skills are invaluable as you move forward, helping you tackle challenges with clarity and calm. In the next chapter, we'll explore decision-making and problem-solving techniques, further equipping you to handle life's complexities confidently.

SUMMARY

This chapter focuses on mastering time management and boosting productivity through practical strategies. Creating a structured daily schedule, setting achievable goals, and incorporating mindfulness can significantly improve focus and reduce stress. Time-blocking, task prioritization, and overcoming procrastination are essential techniques that help you stay organized and efficient. Productivity apps, such as Todoist or Trello, and mindfulness tools, like guided meditation apps, can further optimize your time and maintain balance in work, school, and social life. This holistic approach ensures long-term success and well-being.

CALL TO ACTION ITEMS

1. Create a Daily Schedule: List all your tasks and responsibilities, prioritize them using tools like the Eisenhower Matrix, and allocate specific time slots for each task.
2. Incorporate Mindfulness: Set aside 5–10 minutes daily for mindfulness practices such as breathing, body scan

meditation, or mindful walking to reduce stress and enhance focus.

3. Visual Aid and Tool
   a. Mindfulness Breathing Guide:
      - Breathe in for 4 seconds.
      - Hold your breath for 4 seconds.
      - Exhale for 4 seconds.
      - Repeat for 5–10 minutes.

These tools and practices will help you build a solid time management and mindfulness foundation, leading to enhanced productivity and balance in your life.

7

DECISION-MAKING AND PROBLEM-SOLVING

When my friend Lisa graduated from college, she faced a tough choice. Should she take a high-paying job in a different city, stay close to home, and pursue a passion project with uncertain financial prospects? The decision weighed heavily on her, causing sleepless nights and overwhelming contemplation of the potential outcomes. This scenario is familiar to many young adults. Decisions like choosing a career path, moving to a new city, or even deciding on a major in college can be daunting. However, a structured decision-making approach can bring relief, clarifying and reducing the stress associated with these choices.

7.1 DECISION-MAKING FRAMEWORKS: PROS-AND-CONS LISTS AND SCENARIO PLANNING

Structured decision-making is not just a tool, it's a game-changer. It's the key to making informed and rational choices. By organizing thoughts, reducing emotional bias, and allowing for a better comparison of options, it provides a clear framework for decision-making. When emotions threaten to cloud judgment, a structured approach ensures decisions are based on logic and reason. By systematically evaluating options, you can make choices that align with your long-term goals and values.

Creating effective pros-and-cons lists involves several steps. First, define the decision to be made. Be as specific as possible. For instance, instead of vaguely considering "career options," focus on a particular choice, like "accepting a job offer in another city." Next, list all possible pros and cons. This step requires thorough brainstorming. Write down everything that comes to mind, even if it seems trivial. Weighing the importance of each point is crucial. Not all pros and cons carry the same weight. Assign a value or rank to each item based on how much it matters to you. Finally, make an informed choice based on the pros and cons. This process helps visualize the potential outcomes and make a balanced decision.

Scenario planning is another powerful decision-making tool. It involves creating different future scenarios based on current decisions. This technique allows you to assess potential outcomes and prepare for various possibilities. Start by identifying the decision and then imagine different scenarios that could unfold. For example, if you're deciding whether to move to a new city, consider the best-case scenario (e.g., career advancement, personal growth), the worst-case scenario (e.g., loneliness, financial strain), and the most likely scenario (e.g., a mix of challenges and opportunities). Assess the potential outcomes of each scenario. Think about how each would impact your life, both positively and negatively. Planning for these scenarios helps you prepare for different possibilities, making the decision process less daunting.

Real-life examples illustrate the effectiveness of these frameworks. When choosing a college major, a student might use a pros-and-cons list to compare different fields of study. They could list factors like job prospects, personal interest, and potential earnings for each major. By weighing these factors, they can make a more informed choice. Deciding on a career path is another scenario where these tools are invaluable. For instance, someone considering a career in healthcare versus finance might use scenario planning to envision their future in each field. They could feel the best and worst outcomes, such as job satisfaction, work-life balance, and financial stability, to guide their decision. Planning a significant life change, like moving to a new city, also benefits from these frameworks. By listing the pros and cons of the move and imagining different scenarios, you can make a decision that aligns with your goals and prepares you for potential challenges.

Reflection Section: Applying Decision-Making Tools

Now, let's put these decision-making tools to work. Take a moment to think about a significant decision you're currently facing. It could be related to your career, education, or personal life. Write down the decision and create a pros-and-cons list. List all the factors you can consider and then weigh their importance. Next, use scenario planning to imagine each option's best, worst, and most likely outcomes. Reflect on these scenarios and consider how they impact your decision. This practical exercise will help you gain clarity and confidence in your choice.

By incorporating structured decision-making tools like pros-and-cons lists and scenario planning, you're not just navigating complex decisions but taking control. These frameworks provide a clear path, helping you weigh your options and prepare for various outcomes. Whether choosing a college major, deciding on a career path, or planning a significant life change, these tools empower you to make informed and balanced decisions.

7.2 CRITICAL THINKING: ANALYZING INFORMATION AND MAKING INFORMED CHOICES

When I think about critical thinking, I remember a high school project where we had to research and present on a controversial topic. My friend Anna chose climate change, and while she found tons of information online, she realized that not all of it was reliable. She had to sift through conflicting data, identify credible sources, and present a balanced view. This experience underscored the importance of critical thinking, especially in a world overflowing with information. Critical thinking is essential for making informed decisions because it enhances problem-solving abilities, helps identify biases and assumptions, and promotes logical and objective analysis. By approaching problems with a critical mindset, you can navigate complex situations more effectively and make well-reasoned and justifiable choices, leading to a sense of accomplishment.

Developing critical thinking skills involves several actionable steps. First, start by asking open-ended questions. Ask why, how, and what if instead of seeking simple yes or no answers. These questions encourage exploration and understanding of the underlying issues. Next, evaluate the credibility of sources. Not all information is created equal, so consider the author's qualifications, the publication's reputation, and the evidence provided. Reflecting on personal biases is another crucial step. Everyone has biases that can cloud judgment. Acknowledge these biases and strive to minimize their influence on your decisions. Additionally, consider alternative viewpoints. Exposing yourself to different perspectives broadens your understanding and helps you see the bigger picture.

Analyzing information effectively requires specific techniques. One helpful method is the SWOT analysis, which stands for Strengths, Weaknesses, Opportunities, and Threats. This tool helps break down complex information by categorizing it into these four areas, making it easier to assess and compare options. Fact-checking and cross-referencing data are also vital. Verify the accuracy of information by consulting multiple reputable sources. This step ensures that your decisions are based on reliable and consistent data. Identifying logical fallacies and errors is another crucial technique. Logical fallacies are errors in reasoning that can undermine your arguments. Spotting these fallacies helps you build stronger, more valid arguments.

Practical applications of critical thinking are numerous and varied. When making financial decisions, critical thinking helps you evaluate investment options, assess risks, and make choices that align with your financial goals. Before investing in a stock, you might analyze the company's financial health, market trends, and potential risks. Evaluating job offers is another area where critical thinking is invaluable. Beyond the salary, consider factors like company culture, growth opportunities, and work-life balance. Assessing news articles and media content with a critical eye is also essential. In today's digital age, misinformation is rampant. By critically evaluating the sources and content of news, you can distinguish between credible information and sensationalism.

Reflection Section: Critical Thinking in Action

Think about a recent decision you had to make. It could be related to your education, career, or personal life. Reflect on how you approached the decision. Did you ask open-ended questions? Did you evaluate the credibility of your sources? Consider how applying critical thinking techniques influenced your decision. Write down three steps to strengthen your critical thinking skills in future decisions.

These steps and techniques can enhance your critical thinking abilities and make more informed, logical decisions. Whether you're navigating the complexities of financial decisions, evaluating job offers, or assessing media content, critical thinking provides the tools to analyze information effectively and make reasoned and justifiable choices.

7.3 PROBLEM-SOLVING TECHNIQUES: FROM BRAINSTORMING TO IMPLEMENTATION

Imagine you're tasked with organizing a major event at work. The stakes are high, and failure is not an option. This is where practical problem-solving skills become crucial. These skills enhance creativity and innovation and lead to better outcomes and solutions. In personal and professional settings, tackling problems head-on builds resilience and adaptability, essential traits in today's fast-paced world.

Effective brainstorming is the first step in the problem-solving process. Start by setting a clear problem statement. This helps focus your efforts and ensures everyone understands the issue. Encourage free-flowing ideas without judgment. In this stage, quantity is more important than quality. The goal is to generate as many ideas as possible. Once you have a list of potential solutions, begin categorizing and prioritizing them. Group similar ideas and rank them based on feasibility, impact, and resources required. This organization helps in narrowing down the best options to pursue.

Evaluating and selecting solutions involves several techniques. One effective method is using decision matrices. This tool allows you to compare multiple solutions based on specific criteria, such as cost, time, and effectiveness. Each criterion is weighted according to importance, and solutions are scored accordingly.

Conducting a cost-benefit analysis is another valuable technique. This involves comparing each solution's benefits against its financial and non-financial costs. Consider short-term and long-term impacts when evaluating solutions. A solution that offers immediate relief might not be sustainable eventually, while a more challenging option could provide lasting benefits.

Once a solution is selected, the next step is implementation and monitoring. Develop an action plan with specific tasks and timelines. Break down the solution into manageable steps and assign responsibilities to team members. Clearly outline what needs to be done, by whom, and when. This ensures accountability and keeps the project on track. Assigning resources is also crucial. Ensure that all necessary financial, human, or material resources are available to execute the plan effectively. Regularly review progress and make adjustments as needed. This involves setting up checkpoints to assess how well the solution works and making necessary tweaks to stay on course.

A real-life example of effective problem-solving can be seen in a school setting, where a group of students was tasked with improving recycling efforts. They began by brainstorming various ideas, from awareness campaigns to installing more recycling bins. Using a decision matrix, they evaluated each idea based on cost, potential impact, and ease of implementation. They launched a recycling competition among classes, assigning tasks and timelines for promotion, setup, and monitoring. Through regular reviews and adjustments, they significantly increased recycling rates in their school.

Practical problem-solving is about more than just finding solutions. It's about enhancing creativity, improving outcomes, and building resilience. By mastering techniques like brainstorming, evaluating solutions, and implementing action plans, you can tackle any problem with confidence and efficiency. These skills solve immediate issues and prepare you for future challenges, ensuring continuous personal and professional growth.

7.4 HANDLING UNCERTAINTY: MAKING DECISIONS WITH INCOMPLETE INFORMATION

Imagine you're considering a job offer in a city you've never visited. The role seems promising, but you need to learn more about the area, the company culture, or how the move might impact your personal life. This situation is a classic example of deciding under uncertainty. The challenges of such decisions are numerous. Without complete information, the risk of unexpected outcomes increases, heightening stress and anxiety. You might constantly second-guess your choice, worrying if you made the right call. This uncertainty can lead to regret, especially if things don't pan out as hoped. Navigating these murky waters requires a blend of strategies and a willingness to embrace the unknown.

One effective strategy for managing uncertainty is to seek out as much relevant information as possible. While you may have some answers, gathering data can provide a clearer picture. Reach out to current or former company employees, read reviews about the city, and try to understand the broader economic and social context. Relying on experience and intuition is also valuable. Think back to similar situations where you faced uncertainty. How did you handle them? What worked and what didn't? Your intuition, honed by experiences, can guide you through the ambiguity.

Additionally, using probability and risk assessment can help. Estimate the likelihood of various outcomes and weigh the risks versus the potential rewards. This approach allows you to make a more informed decision, even with incomplete data.

Developing a risk management plan is crucial when dealing with uncertainty. Start by identifying possible risks and their impacts. For instance, if you're considering the job offer, potential risks include job instability, high living costs, or social isolation. Understanding these risks helps you prepare mentally and practically. Creating contingency plans for different scenarios is the next step. If the job doesn't work out, what's your backup plan? Could you return to your current job or find another role quickly? Having these plans in place reduces anxiety and provides a safety net. Regularly updating the risk management plan based on new information is essential. As you gather more data or circumstances change, adjust your plans accordingly. This dynamic approach keeps you prepared for various outcomes.

Successful decision-making under uncertainty can be seen in various real-life cases. Consider entrepreneurs who start new business ventures. They often plunge with limited information, relying on market research, intuition, and risk management strategies. Despite the uncertainties, many thrive by adapting and learning from their experiences. Investing in the stock market is another area rife with uncertainty. Investors make decisions based on trends, historical data, and risk assessments, knowing they can't predict the market with absolute certainty. Yet, many achieve significant returns by balancing risks and rewards. Career changes also exemplify decision-making under uncertainty. Individuals might switch industries or pursue new roles without knowing the exact outcome. They rely on their skills, adaptability, and risk management to navigate the transition successfully.

Handling uncertainty is an inevitable part of life. You can make informed decisions even with incomplete information by seeking relevant information, relying on past experiences and intuition, and using probability and risk assessment. Developing a risk management plan helps anticipate and mitigate potential risks, providing a framework to navigate uncertainties. Real-life examples, from starting new businesses to investing and career changes, demonstrate that effective decision-making under uncertainty is achievable with the right strategies and mindset.

7.5 LEARNING FROM MISTAKES: TURNING FAILURES INTO OPPORTUNITIES

Not long ago, my friend Emily decided to launch her own business. She poured her heart and soul into it, but things didn't go as planned. The company struggled, and eventually, she had to shut it down. Despite the initial disappointment, Emily viewed this failure as a valuable learning experience. Mistakes, as painful as they can be, provide insights for future improvement. They offer a unique perspective that success rarely does. Mistakes build resilience and adaptability, teaching you to navigate challenges and bounce back stronger. They also encourage a growth mindset, which values learning and development over static perfection.

To truly learn from mistakes, you need a structured approach. Start by identifying what went wrong and why. This isn't about assigning blame but understanding the root cause. Reflect on the sequence of events and pinpoint the decisions or actions that led to the mistake. Next, acknowledge personal responsibility. Owning your part in the failure is crucial for growth. It's easy to blame external factors, but recognizing your role allows you to control and change your future actions. Extract critical lessons and insights from the experience. What did the mistake teach you? How can you apply these lessons to avoid similar pitfalls in the future? Finally, use these lessons in future decisions. Adjust your strategies, processes, or mindset based on your learning.

Fostering a growth mindset is essential for turning mistakes into opportunities. One effective strategy is viewing challenges as opportunities to learn. Instead of seeing a mistake as a setback, frame it as a stepping stone to growth. Celebrate progress and effort, not just outcomes. Acknowledge the hard work and dedication you put into your efforts, regardless of the result. This reinforces the idea that learning and growing is valuable in itself. Seek feedback and use it constructively. Ask for input from mentors, peers, or experts, and use their insights to improve. Constructive feedback provides different perspectives and helps you see areas for improvement that you might have missed.

There are countless stories of individuals who turned their failures into valuable lessons. Take entrepreneurs who learned from failed startups. Many successful business owners faced initial failures but used those experiences to refine their ideas and approach. For example, the founders of Airbnb faced multiple rejections before their idea took off. They learned from each setback, made necessary adjustments, and eventually built a thriving business. Professionals who bounce back from career setbacks also exemplify this principle. Consider a marketing executive who lost their job due to a failed campaign. Instead of giving up, they analyzed what went wrong, sought additional training, and landed a new role where they applied their newfound knowledge to achieve more tremendous success. Students who improve after academic failures provide another powerful example. A student struggling with failing grades might seek tutoring, develop better study habits, and achieve academic excellence.

Reflection Section: Learning from Personal Mistakes

Think about a recent mistake you made. Reflect on what went wrong and why. Write down the key lessons you learned from this experience. Consider how you can apply these lessons to future decisions or actions. This exercise will help you internalize the insights gained and use them to foster continuous improvement.

Embracing mistakes as learning opportunities transforms how you approach challenges. By analyzing and learning from errors, fostering a growth mindset, and applying these lessons to future endeavors, you can turn failures into stepping stones for success. The stories of entrepreneurs, professionals, and students who have done so serve as powerful reminders that mistakes are not the end but a crucial part of the path to growth and achievement.

7.6 SEEKING ADVICE: WHEN AND HOW TO ASK FOR HELP

Imagine staring at a job offer that could change your life but still determining if it's the right move. You feel the weight of the decision pressing on your shoulders. This is where seeking advice becomes invaluable. Asking for help brings additional perspectives and insights you might have yet to consider. It reduces the risk of blind spots and biases that can cloud your judgment. When you're emotionally invested in a decision, it's easy to miss critical aspects. Consulting others can provide a more balanced view and offer emotional support, giving you the confidence to move forward.

Identifying suitable sources of advice is crucial. Not all advice is created equal, so finding reliable and knowledgeable advisors is essential. Mentors and professional networks are excellent resources. With their experience and expertise, mentors can provide guidance tailored to your situation. Professional networks, such as industry associations or alums groups, can offer diverse perspectives. Subject-matter experts are another valuable source. These individuals have specialized knowledge in specific areas, making their insights particularly relevant for technical or complex decisions. Trusted friends and family members also play a crucial role. They know you well and can offer advice aligning with your values and goals.

Approaching others for advice requires clear communication. Start by being specific about the decision or problem you're facing. Instead of vaguely saying, "I need help with my career," clarify, "I'm considering a job offer in a new city and need advice on whether it's the right move." This specificity helps advisors provide targeted and relevant insights. Asking open-ended questions encourages more in-depth discussion. Questions like, "What do you think are the pros and cons of this decision?" or "How would you approach this situation?" invite expansive and thoughtful responses. Showing appreciation for their time and insights is also essential. A simple thank you, or a follow-up gratitude message reinforces your value of their advice and encourages future support.

Incorporating external advice into your decision-making process involves several steps. Weigh the advice against your values and goals. Not all advice will align with your unique circumstances, so it's essential to filter suggestions through the lens of what matters most to you. Consider the feasibility and practicality of the advice. Given your resources or constraints, some suggestions sound great in theory but may need to be more practical. Evaluate how realistic and actionable the advice is within your specific context. Finally, the final decision will be made based on a balanced perspective. Synthesize the advice you've received with your analysis and intuition. This integrated approach ensures that your decision is well-rounded and informed.

For example, you're contemplating pursuing further education or entering the workforce. You might seek advice from a mentor who has navigated both paths, a subject-matter expert who understands the industry demands, and a trusted friend who knows your aspirations. You gather a range of insights by articulating your dilemma and asking open-ended questions. Weighing these against your career goals and personal circumstances, gaining work experience first aligns better with your immediate objectives while keeping further education open for the future.

Seeking advice is about finding answers and enriching your decision-making process. By gaining diverse perspectives, reducing biases, and receiving emotional support, you can navigate complex decisions with greater clarity and confidence. Identifying reliable sources, communicating effectively, and incorporating advice into your final decision ensures that you make well-rounded and informed choices. Whether it's a career move, a personal decision, or any significant choice, asking for help can be the key to making the best possible decision.

SUMMARY

This chapter introduces decision-making frameworks and problem-solving techniques to help young adults make rational decisions. It highlights the importance of structured decision-making tools like pros-and-cons lists, scenario planning, critical thinking, and problem-solving strategies. These tools provide a clear path for weighing options and considering different outcomes. The chapter also discusses handling uncertainty, learning from mistakes, and seeking advice.

CALL TO ACTION

- Step 1: When faced with an important decision, create a pros-and-cons list and use scenario planning to evaluate the potential outcomes of each option.
- Step 2: Apply critical thinking by asking open-ended

questions and evaluating the credibility of sources before making a decision.

Examples:

- Choosing a Career Path: Use a pros-and-cons list to compare job offers and scenario planning to visualize different outcomes.
- Investment Decisions: Apply critical thinking to analyze market trends and company performance before investing.

KEY POINTS:

- Structured decision-making reduces emotional bias and provides clarity.
- Critical thinking helps evaluate information and recognize biases.
- Problem-solving techniques guide brainstorming and solution implementation.
- Handling uncertainty requires balancing risks with incomplete information.
- Learning from mistakes promotes growth and resilience.

Visual Aids or Tools:

- Example Pros-and-Cons List: A visual representation of weighing career options.
- Scenario Planning Flowchart: Illustrates different possible outcomes of a decision.
- SWOT Analysis Chart: Helps break down a complex decision.

8

PERSONAL GROWTH AND SELF-DISCOVERY

Self-reflection, a potent tool for personal growth, offers a profound understanding of your strengths and weaknesses. By exploring your thoughts, feelings, actions, and motivations, you gain invaluable insights that steer your career and personal decisions. This heightened self-awareness enhances your emotional intelligence, empowering you to handle situations with more empathy and understanding. Furthermore, self-reflection forms a robust foundation for setting achievable goals as you become more cognizant of your areas of excellence and areas for improvement.

Journaling, a potent technique for self-reflection, allows you to delve deeper into your daily experiences and emotions. This practice aids in identifying patterns in your behavior and thought processes, making it easier to comprehend what motivates you and where you might need to make changes. For instance, if you often feel stressed after certain activities, journaling can help you pinpoint the cause and consider how to address it. Seeking feedback from trusted individuals can provide valuable perspectives that you might overlook on your own. Friends, family, and mentors can offer insights into your strengths and weaknesses, helping you see yourself from different angles. Self-assessment tools and quizzes are also helpful in gaining a clearer understanding of your personality traits and skills. These tools can highlight areas where you excel and suggest effective leveraging of these strengths.

Recognizing and leveraging your strengths can significantly enhance your personal and professional life. Reflect on past successes and achievements to identify your core strengths. For instance, if you've consistently received praise for your problem-solving abilities, consider how this skill can be applied in different contexts. Aligning your strengths with career opportunities and hobbies can lead to greater satisfaction and success. Project management or event planning roles might be a good fit if you excel at organizing and planning. Creating a personal strengths inventory—a detailed list of your skills, talents, and attributes— can be valuable when making career decisions or setting goals. This inventory boosts your confidence and provides a clear picture of what you bring to the table.

Addressing and improving weaknesses is equally essential for personal growth. Start by setting specific, actionable improvement goals. For instance, if you need help with public speaking, set a goal to practice speaking in front of small groups and gradually increase the audience size. Seek resources and training to build skills where you need more confidence. Online courses, workshops, and coaching can provide the guidance and support you need to improve. Practicing self-compassion and patience is crucial during this process. Recognize that everyone has weaknesses and that improvement takes time and effort. Avoid harsh self-criticism and instead focus on incremental progress. Celebrate small victories along the way, as these successes can motivate you to continue working on your weaknesses.

Reflection Exercise: Creating Your Strengths Inventory

Take a moment to list your top five strengths. Reflect on how these strengths have helped you in the past and how they can be applied to your current goals. Next, identify two areas where you feel you need improvement. Write down specific actions you can take to address these weaknesses and set a timeline for achieving these goals. This exercise will help you understand your abilities and create a personalized growth plan.

Self-reflection and self-discipline are not just processes, they are journeys of empowerment and continuous learning. By regularly assessing your strengths and weaknesses, and by cultivating self-discipline, you can make informed decisions, set realistic goals, and navigate the complexities of life with greater confidence and ease. You are in control, and you are capable of achieving your goals.

8.1 BUILDING SELF-DISCIPLINE: CREATING HABITS FOR SUCCESS

Imagine waking up each day with a clear sense of purpose. Your goals and tasks are set, and you move through your day with focus and efficiency. This sense of control and productivity is primarily thanks to self-discipline. It's the backbone of personal and professional achievement. When you cultivate self-discipline, you enhance your ability to focus and maintain productivity, even in the face of challenges. It enables you to stick to your long-term goals, building resilience and perseverance. Without self-discipline, it's easy to get sidetracked by distractions or give up when things get tough.

Developing self-discipline starts with setting clear, achievable targets. It's important to know exactly what you're working towards. Whether getting fit, saving money, or advancing your career, your goals should be specific and realistic. Breaking tasks into manageable steps can make even the most daunting goals feel more attainable. For example, if you want to write a book, start by setting a daily word count target instead of focusing on the entire manuscript. Using positive reinforcement and rewards can also motivate you to stay disciplined. Reward yourself for reaching milestones, no matter how small. This could be a treat, a break, or anything that makes you feel good about your progress.

Creating and maintaining successful habits is crucial for sustaining self-discipline. Begin by identifying habits that align with your personal goals. Habits like regular exercise and balanced eating are essential to improve your health. Habit-tracking tools and apps can help you stay accountable. Apps like Habitica or Streaks turn habit-tracking into a game, making it more engaging and fun. Establishing routines and rituals can also reinforce discipline. Having a morning routine, for instance, sets a positive tone for the rest of the day. These routines don't have to be elaborate; simple actions like making bed, meditating for a few minutes, or planning your day can make a significant difference.

Overcoming common obstacles to self-discipline is part of the journey. Managing distractions and time-wasters is essential. Identify what tends to divert your attention—social media, TV, or even specific people—and find ways to minimize these distractions. For instance, you can use apps that block distracting websites during work hours or designate specific times for checking your phone. Dealing with procrastination and lack of motivation can be challenging but not impossible. One effective strategy is the "two-minute rule." If a task will take less than two minutes, do it immediately. This approach helps you overcome the inertia of starting. Seeking accountability from peers or mentors can also boost self-discipline. Share your goals with someone who can provide encouragement and hold you accountable. Regular check-ins with this person can help you stay on track and make adjustments as needed.

Self-Discipline Exercise: Daily Diligence Tracker

Create a daily diligence tracker to monitor your progress. List your critical daily tasks and check them off as you complete them. This simple exercise provides a sense of accomplishment and helps you identify patterns and areas for improvement. Seeing your progress visually can motivate and reinforce your commitment to your goals, making you feel motivated and accomplished.

Building self-discipline is a continuous process that requires dedication and effort. By setting clear targets, breaking tasks into manageable steps, and using positive reinforcement, you can cultivate habits that align with your goals. Overcoming distractions and procrastination and seeking accountability further strengthen your discipline.

8.2 PURSUING PASSIONS: FINDING AND CULTIVATING YOUR INTERESTS

Imagine waking up with excitement and purpose every day, knowing you're about to engage in activities that ignite your enthusiasm. Pursuing your passions contributes significantly to your overall well-being. It enhances life satisfaction and happiness, providing a sense of purpose and direction that can make life's mundane aspects more meaningful. Engaging in passion encourages creativity and innovation, helping you think outside the box and approach problems from new angles. Think of passions as the fuel that powers your drive and determination, making life not just a series of tasks but a fulfilling experience.

Identifying your passions and interests might seem daunting, but it's rewarding. Start by reflecting on your childhood interests and hobbies. What activities did you gravitate towards naturally? These early interests can explain your passions, whether drawing, playing a musical instrument, or exploring nature. Next, explore new activities and experiences. Take a cooking class, join a hiking club, or try your hand at writing. Sometimes, you discover a passion by stepping out of your comfort zone and trying something new. Personality and interest assessments can also be incredibly insightful. Tools like the Myers-Briggs Type Indicator (MBTI) or the Strong Interest Inventory can help you understand your preferences and suggest activities that align with your personality.

Once you've identified your passions, the next step is to cultivate and nurture them. Set aside dedicated time each week to focus on your interests. This could be as simple as blocking out an hour every Saturday morning for painting or dedicating your lunch breaks to learning a new language. Seeking out learning opportunities and resources is also crucial. Enroll in online courses, attend workshops, or read books related to your passion. The more you immerse yourself in the subject, the deeper your connection will grow. Connecting with communities and groups with similar interests can provide support and inspiration. Join local clubs, attend meetups, or participate in online forums. These communities can offer valuable feedback, encouragement, and shared experiences that enrich your pursuit.

Balancing passions with other responsibilities can be challenging but is entirely possible with some planning. Prioritize and time-block your passions into your schedule. Treat these blocks of time as non-negotiable appointments with yourself. Combining your passions with your career or education can also be practical. For instance, if you're passionate about environmental conservation, seek out careers in sustainability or volunteer for related projects.

Setting realistic expectations and goals is essential. Understand that you may not be able to devote as much time to your passion as you'd like, especially if you have other significant responsibilities. Set small, achievable goals that fit your current lifestyle and gradually build from there.

Reflect on how pursuing your passions has impacted your life. Has it made you feel more fulfilled? Do you find yourself more energized and motivated? Write down your observations and consider ways to integrate your passions into your daily routine fully. Pursuing passions isn't just about filling your free time; it's about enriching your life and fostering a sense of purpose and joy.

8.3 DEVELOPING RESILIENCE: OVERCOMING CHALLENGES AND SETBACKS

Imagine facing a significant setback, like failing a crucial exam or losing a job you loved. The immediate reaction might be despair or frustration, but resilience helps you bounce back and move forward. Resilience is vital for navigating life's challenges because it builds emotional strength and perseverance. When you cultivate resilience, you enhance your ability to adapt to new situations and solve problems effectively. This adaptability allows you to face difficulties head-on and emerge stronger, turning potential obstacles into opportunities for growth.

Building resilience involves several practical techniques. Practicing gratitude and positive thinking can significantly impact your mindset. By focusing on what you have rather than your lack, you shift your perspective to a more optimistic one. This doesn't mean ignoring problems but approaching them with a mindset that seeks solutions and recognizes small victories. Mindfulness and stress-reduction techniques, such as deep breathing exercises or meditation, can help you manage stress and maintain emotional balance. These practices allow you to stay present, reducing anxiety about the future or regret about the past. Seeking support from friends, family, or counselors is another crucial aspect of building resilience. Surrounding yourself with a supportive network provides emotional comfort and practical advice, helping you navigate challenging times with a sense of community and shared strength.

Turning challenges into opportunities for growth requires a shift in perspective. When faced with a setback, take the time to analyze what can be learned from the experience. This reflective process helps you gain insights to inform future decisions and actions. Setting new goals based on these insights can provide a sense of direction and purpose, motivating you to move forward. Celebrate small victories, recognizing that progress often comes in incremental steps rather than giant leaps. These celebrations boost your morale and reinforce positive behaviors and attitudes, contributing to resilience.

Real-life examples of resilience can be incredibly inspiring. Consider entrepreneurs who have rebuilt their businesses after experiencing significant failures. They often cite these setbacks as pivotal moments that taught them valuable lessons and ultimately led to tremendous success. For instance, Steve Jobs was famously ousted from Apple, the company he co-founded, only to return years later and transform it into one of the most successful companies in the world. Athletes who recover from injuries to achieve success also exemplify resilience. Take Bethany Hamilton, a surfer who lost her arm in a shark attack but continued to compete at the highest levels, inspiring millions with her determination and grit. Students who overcome academic struggles to excel demonstrate that resilience in the face of failure can lead to remarkable achievements. For example, Albert Einstein struggled in school but went on to revolutionize physics with his theories.

Resilience is not just about bouncing back; it's about growing stronger through adversity. By practicing gratitude, mindfulness, and seeking support, you can develop a resilient mindset that helps you navigate life's challenges confidently and gracefully. Analyzing setbacks and celebrating small victories further reinforce your ability to turn difficulties into opportunities for growth. The stories of resilient individuals across various fields are potent reminders that setbacks are not the end but a stepping stone toward more significant achievements.

8.4 EMBRACING CHANGE: ADAPTING TO LIFE'S TRANSITIONS

Change is an inevitable part of life, and adapting to it is crucial for continuous development. Embracing change promotes flexibility and open-mindedness, encouraging you to step outside your comfort zone and explore new possibilities. This adaptability facilitates new opportunities and experiences, enriching your personal and professional life. Whether it's a career change, moving to a new city, or adjusting to significant personal life changes like marriage or parenthood, navigating transitions smoothly can significantly improve your overall well-being.

To embrace and manage change effectively, maintain a positive and proactive attitude. Viewing change as an opportunity rather than a threat can help you approach transitions with enthusiasm and curiosity. Setting realistic expectations and goals is also essential. Understand that change often comes with challenges, and taking small, manageable steps toward adapting is okay. Seeking support and guidance from others can provide valuable perspectives and emotional comfort. Talk to friends, family, or mentors who have gone through similar experiences, and learn from their insights and advice.

Planning for major life transitions can make the process more manageable. Create a transition plan with clear steps outlining what needs to be done and when. This plan can serve as a roadmap, guiding you through each transition phase and helping you stay focused and organized. Building a support network is equally important. Surround yourself with people who can offer emotional support, practical assistance, and encouragement. Practicing self-care during stressful periods can help you maintain your physical and emotional well-being. Activities like exercise, meditation, and hobbies can provide a much-needed break and help you recharge.

Examples of successful adaptation to change can offer inspiration and practical insights. Consider individuals who have thrived through significant life transitions, such as career changes and job relocations. For instance, Sheryl Sandberg transitioned from working at the U.S. Treasury to becoming the COO of Facebook, navigating a significant career shift with grace and resilience. Moving to a new city or country can also be a transformative experience. People like Trevor Noah, who moved from South Africa to the United States, have successfully adapted to new environments, embracing the opportunities and challenges of such a move. Adjusting to significant personal life changes, like marriage or parenthood, requires flexibility and open-mindedness. Couples who navigate these transitions successfully often emphasize the importance of communication, mutual support, and maintaining a sense of humor.

Embracing change and adapting to life's transitions is a continuous process. You can navigate these changes confidently and resiliently by maintaining a positive attitude, setting realistic goals, seeking support, and practicing self-care. The stories of individuals who have successfully adapted to significant life transitions are potent reminders that change, while challenging, can lead to growth, new opportunities, and a more prosperous, more fulfilling life.

8.5 SETTING AND ACHIEVING PERSONAL GOALS: MAPPING YOUR FUTURE

Setting and achieving personal goals is a crucial aspect of personal development, providing direction and motivation. Setting clear, actionable goals enhances self-confidence and accomplishment, facilitating continuous growth and improvement. Goals act as a roadmap, guiding you toward your desired future and helping you stay focused and motivated.

Effective goal-setting involves using practical methods that ensure your goals are meaningful and achievable. The SMART goal framework is a widely used approach that encourages you to set Specific, Measurable, Achievable, Relevant, and Time-bound goals. This framework helps you create clear and detailed goals, making tracking progress and staying on course easier. Breaking down long-term goals into short-term tasks can make the process more manageable. For example, if your long-term goal is to run a marathon, start by setting short-term goals like running a certain distance each week. Regularly reviewing and adjusting your goals ensures they align with your evolving priorities and circumstances.

A personal development plan can provide a structured approach to achieving your goals. Start by identifying critical areas for growth and improvement. This could include career advancement, personal relationships, health, or hobbies. Set specific, measurable milestones for each location, and create a timeline for achieving these goals. This plan serves as a roadmap, helping you stay focused and organized.

Overcoming obstacles to goal achievement is part of the process. Staying motivated through setbacks can be challenging, but it's essential to maintain your commitment. Seek accountability from mentors or peers who can provide encouragement and hold you accountable. Regular check-ins with an accountability partner can help you stay on track and make necessary adjustments. Celebrating progress and accomplishments, no matter how small, can also boost your motivation and reinforce positive behaviors.

Reflect on your progress and consider how your goals have evolved. Adjust your plan to stay aligned with your current priorities and circumstances. Regular reflection and adjustment ensure that your goals remain relevant and attainable, helping you stay focused and motivated on your path to personal growth and success.

8.6 EMBRACING CHANGE: ADAPTING TO LIFE'S TRANSITIONS

Change is an inevitable part of life, and adapting to it is crucial for continuous development. When you learn to embrace change, you promote flexibility and open-mindedness. This helps you grow outside your comfort zone and facilitates new opportunities and experiences. Being adaptable makes these transitions smoother and more manageable, whether starting a new job, moving to a different city, or adjusting to a significant change in your personal life.

Maintaining a positive and proactive attitude is essential when facing change. Instead of fearing the unknown, change should be viewed as an opportunity for growth. Setting realistic expectations and goals can also help you navigate transitions more effectively. Understand that change often comes with challenges, and taking things one step at a time is okay. Seeking support and guidance from others can provide valuable insights and emotional comfort. Friends, family, and mentors can offer advice and share their experiences, helping you feel less alone during times of transition.

Planning for major life transitions involves several practical steps. Start by creating a transition plan with clear steps outlining what needs to be done and when. This plan can serve as a roadmap, guiding you through each transition phase and helping you stay focused and organized. Building a support network is equally important. Surround yourself with people who can offer emotional support, practical assistance, and encouragement. Practicing self-care during stressful periods can help you maintain your physical and emotional well-being. Activities like exercise, meditation, and hobbies can provide a much-needed break and help you recharge.

Consider the story of Ava, who made a significant career change from marketing to teaching. She faced initial challenges, including adjusting to a new work environment and learning new skills. However, she successfully transitioned into her new role by maintaining a positive attitude, seeking support from colleagues and mentors, and setting realistic goals. Similarly, think about Miguel, who moved to a new country for a job opportunity. The cultural differences and language barriers were initially daunting, but he adapted and thrived by building a support network and embracing the new culture.

Another example is Sarah and James, who recently got married. They had to adjust to living together and balancing their careers and responsibilities. By communicating openly, setting shared goals, and supporting each other, they navigated this significant personal life change smoothly.

Adapting to change is a continuous process that involves maintaining a positive attitude, setting realistic goals, seeking support, and practicing self-care. By following these strategies, you can navigate life's transitions with confidence and resilience, turning challenges into opportunities for growth and new experiences.

8.7 SETTING AND ACHIEVING PERSONAL GOALS: MAPPING YOUR FUTURE

Setting and achieving personal goals is a cornerstone of long-term success and personal development. When you establish clear goals, you provide yourself with direction and motivation. This clarity helps you focus on what truly matters, making your efforts more targeted and effective. The sense of accomplishment from achieving your goals enhances your self-confidence, reinforcing your belief in your abilities. Moreover, setting and working towards goals facilitates continuous growth and improvement, constantly pushing you to evolve and improve yourself.

The SMART goal framework is one practical method for setting meaningful and achievable goals. This approach encourages you to make your goals Specific, Measurable, Achievable, Relevant, and Time-bound. For instance, instead of setting a vague goal like "get fit," you might set a SMART goal such as "run three miles, three times a week for the next two months." This goal is specific, measurable, achievable, relevant to fitness, and has a clear time-frame. Breaking down long-term goals into short-term tasks makes them more manageable and less overwhelming. If your long-term goal is to write a book, set daily or weekly word count targets. Regularly reviewing and adjusting your goals ensures they align with your current priorities and circumstances. Life is dynamic, and your goals should be flexible enough to adapt to changes in your situation or aspirations.

Creating a personal development plan involves several actionable steps. Begin by identifying critical areas for growth and improvement. These areas include career advancement, personal relationships, health, and hobbies. Once you know where to improve, set specific, measurable milestones for each location. For example, if you want to advance in your career, a milestone might be to complete a professional certification within six months. Creating a timeline for achieving these goals helps you stay organized and focused. This timeline acts as a roadmap, guiding you through each step of your personal development journey.

Overcoming obstacles to goal achievement is an inevitable part of the process. Staying motivated through setbacks can be challenging, but it's essential to maintain your commitment. One way to stay motivated is by seeking accountability from mentors or peers. Sharing your goals with someone who can provide encouragement and hold you accountable increases your chances of success. Regular check-ins with this person can help you stay on track and make necessary adjustments. Celebrating progress and accomplishments, no matter how small, can also boost your motivation and reinforce positive behaviors. Recognize and reward yourself for your effort, even if you have not reached the final goal.

Reflect on your progress and consider how your goals have evolved. Adjust your plan to stay aligned with your current priorities and circumstances. Regular reflection and adjustment ensure that your goals remain relevant and attainable, helping you stay focused and motivated on your path to personal growth and success. Setting, working towards, and achieving goals enables you to accomplish specific objectives and fosters a mindset of continuous improvement and resilience.

As you navigate the complexities of personal growth and self-discovery, remember that each step brings you closer to understanding and fulfilling your potential. This journey is about achieving milestones and growing into the person you aspire to be. With a clear sense of direction, resilience, and the right tools, you can create a fulfilling and successful life.

Summary: Personal growth and self-discovery stem from ongoing self-reflection, awareness of strengths and weaknesses, and a commitment to setting and achieving personal goals. By practicing techniques such as journaling and feedback seeking, you can gain valuable insights into your character and motivations. Leveraging your strengths in career and life decisions can enhance satisfaction and success. At the same time, improving weaknesses by setting actionable improvement goals helps ensure continuous growth. Building self-discipline, resilience, and adaptability further equip you to navigate life's challenges and transitions, ultimately leading to a more fulfilling, purpose-driven life.

CALL TO ACTION:

- Begin a Self-Reflection Practice: Journal daily or weekly to better understand your thoughts, feelings, and motivations.
- Set a Growth Goal: Identify one strength you can leverage more effectively and one weakness to improve, then create a clear, actionable plan for both.

Reference to Bar Mitzvah/Bat Mitzvah: The importance of rites of passage, like a Bar Mitzvah or Bat Mitzvah, emphasizes the role of self-reflection, growth, and transition into adulthood. These ceremonies symbolize the importance of responsibility and the awareness of one's strengths and potential in the community. Personal development and self-discovery reflect similar transitions as individuals embrace new life phases with increased self-awareness and purpose.

Recommended Tools:

- Journaling apps (e.g., Day One).
- Strengths assessments (e.g., StrengthsFinder, MBTI).
- Daily habit-tracking tools (e.g., Habitica, Streaks).
- Feedback from mentors or trusted individuals for broader perspectives.

These tools and strategies provide practical ways to foster personal growth, whether you're working toward individual goals, overcoming challenges, or building a resilient mindset to navigate life's inevitable transitions.

CONCLUSION

As you reach the end of "Essential Life Skills for Young Adults: Learn the Skills You Need for Independence, Confidence, and Success in the Real World," it's time to reflect on our journey together. We've covered many topics to equip you with the skills necessary for a successful and fulfilling adult life. From financial literacy and career readiness to personal growth and emotional intelligence, each chapter has been a step toward mastering the complexities of the real world.

Throughout this book, we've emphasized the importance of practical guidance and decision-making frameworks. These tools aren't just theoretical concepts but actionable steps to navigate life's challenges confidently. Much like the transformative experiences of a Bar mitzvah or a quinceañera, this book aims to be a rite of passage, empowering you to step into adulthood with a sense of preparedness and self-assurance.

One of the key takeaways from our exploration is the importance of financial literacy. Understanding how to budget, manage credit, and invest are foundational skills that will serve you well throughout your life. We also delved into career readiness, offering tips on crafting standout resumes, acing job interviews, and building professional networks. These skills are crucial for securing and thriving in your chosen career path.

Health and wellness were also focal points, highlighting the significance of meal planning, fitness, and mental health. By adopting these practices, you can maintain a balanced and healthy lifestyle, ensuring that your career success does not come at the expense of your well-being. Emotional intelligence and relationship skills are equally important, helping you build solid and meaningful connections with others while managing conflicts effectively.

Practical life skills like home maintenance, car care, and understanding legal documents should be considered. These skills save you money and give you a sense of independence and competence. Time management and productivity strategies ensure you can juggle multiple responsibilities without feeling overwhelmed, while decision-making and problem-solving techniques help you quickly navigate uncertainties.

Now, it's time for you to take action. Reflect on the lessons and skills we've discussed. Identify areas where you can start implementing changes immediately. Whether setting up a budget, planning your meals for the week, or updating your resume, small steps can significantly improve your life.

Remember, this journey is ongoing. Personal growth and self-discovery have yet to have a final destination. They are continuous processes that evolve as you do. Embrace the challenges and opportunities that come your way. Use the skills and knowledge you've gained to make informed decisions, build strong relationships, and lead a balanced, fulfilling life. This ongoing nature of personal growth should inspire and motivate you, knowing that there's always room for improvement and new experiences.

I want to leave you with an inspiring thought: You have the power to shape your future. Every skill you learn, every decision you make, and every challenge you overcome contributes to the person you are becoming. Believe in your potential, stay curious, and never stop learning.

I am grateful for the opportunity to share this journey with you. Your commitment to personal growth and learning is commendable. Your dedication to improving yourself and your life has not gone unnoticed. As you move forward, remember that you are not alone. There are countless resources, mentors, and communities ready to support you.

Thank you for allowing me to be a part of your journey. Your trust and engagement with the skills and insights from this book have been invaluable. May they serve you well as you navigate the exciting and sometimes daunting path of adulthood. Here's to your independence, confidence, and success in the real world.

In closing, let me leave you with this:

The Harvard Business School study on goal setting, often referred to in personal development and business contexts, examined the impact of written goals on success. While the exact details of this "study" have sometimes been misrepresented in famous self-help circles, the most common version of the story describes research that supposedly found:

- 3% of people who wrote down clear goals were significantly more successful than those who didn't set clear goals.
- 13% of participants had goals in mind but had yet to write them down. They achieved moderate success.
- 84% had no specific goals and achieved the slightest success.

While this "study" is frequently cited in books and seminars, there's no formal record of Harvard conducting it or publishing any findings. However, the general principle it conveys—that setting and writing down clear, actionable goals leads to higher levels of achievement—is supported by broader research in goal-setting psychology.

Studies in goal-setting theory, such as those by Edwin Locke and Gary Latham, support the idea that clear, specific, and challenging goals, combined with consistent feedback and commitment, tend to result in higher performance in various areas of life. Writing down goals reinforces commitment, provides clarity, and is a visual reminder of what you want to achieve.

So, while the specific Harvard Business School study might be more anecdotal than factual, the principle it represents aligns with well-established psychological research on the importance of goal setting in driving success.

REFERENCES

Financial Literacy: What It Is, and Why It Is So Important To ... https://www.investopedia.com/terms/f/financial-literacy.asp

Best Budgeting Apps Of September 2024 https://www.forbes.com/advisor/banking/best-budgeting-apps/

How do I get and keep a good credit score? https://www.consumerfinance.gov/ask-cfpb/how-do-i-get-and-keep-a-good-credit-score-en-318/

7 Best Micro-Investing Apps for 2024 https://millennialmoneyman.com/micro-investing/

How To Write Cover Letters That Stand Out (With Example) https://www.indeed.com/career-advice/resumes-cover-letters/cover-letters-that-stand-out

50+ Most Common Interview Questions and Answers https://www.themuse.com/advice/interview-questions-and-answers

Essential Networking Strategies for Young Professionals to ... https://www.socialmediabutterflyblog.com/2024/04/essential-networking-strategies-for-young-professionals-to-build-lasting-career-connections/

The 4 Things You Need to Thrive in the Gig Economy https://hbr.org/2018/03/thriving-in-the-gig-economy

Meal Prep Guide - The Nutrition Source https://nutritionsource.hsph.harvard.edu/meal-prep/

Nine ideas for creating a budget-friendly workout routine https://www.utdailybeacon.com/arts_and_culture/lifestyle/9-ideas-for-creating-a-budget-friendly-workout-routine/article_000cf672-f1cb-11ee-b7ac-b7780aa1d85b.html

Stress symptoms: Effects on your body and behavior https://www.mayoclinic.org/healthy-lifestyle/stress-management/in-depth/stress-symptoms/art-20050987

How to create a self-care plan personalized to your needs: https://www.calm.com/blog/self-care-plan

The Power of Emotional Intelligence in Relationships https://care-clinics.com/the-power-of-emotional-intelligence-in-relationships/#:~

Effective Communication: Improving Your Interpersonal Skills https://www.helpguide.org/relationships/communication/effective-communication

Conflict management with pre-teens and teenagers https://raisingchildren.net.au/teens/communicating-relationships/communicating/conflict-management-with-teens

Bar Mitzvahs, Quinceañeras, and Confirmations https://2dadswithbaggage.com/bar-mitzvahs-quinceaneras-and-confirmations/

The Ultimate Home Maintenance Checklist for Every Season https://www.bhg.com/home-improvement/advice/home-maintenance-checklist/

The Ultimate Car Maintenance Checklist https://www.bridgestonetire.com/learn/maintenance/ultimate-car-maintenance-checklist/

First Time Apartment Renter's Guide: 20-Step Checklist https://www.apartmentlist.com/renter-life/first-time-renter-apartment-guide-checklist

Preparing Young Adults for the Legal Realities of Life https://www.rocketlawyer.com/family-and-personal/legal-guide/how-to-prepare-young-adults-for-lifes-legal-realities

13 Practical Time Management Skills To Teach Teens https://lifeskillsadvocate.com/blog/13-practical-time-management-skills-to-teach-teens/

Daily Routines and Habits of Successful People https://clockify.me/daily-routines-habits-productive-people

5 Research-Based Strategies for Overcoming Procrastination https://hbr.org/2017/10/5-research-based-strategies-for-overcoming-procrastination

Top 10 best productivity apps for students https://uwaterloo.ca/future-students/missing-manual/high-school/top-10-best-productivity-apps-students

Youth--Social Competencies; Decision-Making https://cales.arizona.edu/sfcs/cyfernet/nowg/sc_decision.html

How to Develop Critical Thinking Skills in 7 Steps ... https://asana.com/resources/critical-thinking-skills

Teaching The IDEAL Problem-Solving Method To Diverse ... https://lifeskillsadvocate.com/blog/teaching-the-ideal-problem-solving-method-to-diverse-learners/

Managing uncertainty: Principles for improved decision ... https://www.cambridge.org/core/services/aop-cambridge-core/content/view/12F3720B113D2991BDE1B8172292B565/S135732172000015Xa.pdf/managing_uncertainty_principles_for_improved_decision_making.pdf

Self-Reflection: Benefits and How to Practice https://www.verywellmind.com/self-reflection-importance-benefits-and-strategies-7500858

9 Powerful Ways To Cultivate Extreme Self-Discipline https://www.forbes.com/sites/brentgleeson/2020/08/25/8-powerful-ways-to-cultivate-extreme-self-discipline/

How to Find Your Passion and Discover Your Zest for Life https://www.betterup.com/blog/how-to-find-your-passion

8 Examples of Resilience in Life and Business From Real ... https://resilientstories.com/examples-of-resilience/

Made in United States
Orlando, FL
15 December 2024

55752391R00085